SUPERNATURAL
(the normal christian life)

WENDY MANN

malcolm down
PUBLISHING

'This is a great book that combines biblical teaching with first-hand experience, encouraging each of us to step up and step out when it comes to being naturally supernatural. It highlights how everyday acts of obedience by normal people can lead to the Kingdom of God breaking through and features many moving and inspiring answers to prayer.'
Mike Pilavachi, Leader of Soul Survivor ministries, a charity that aims to equip young people to live their lives for Jesus, international speaker.

'Wendy incarnates the message she brings in Naturally Supernatural. She is among the first of a new generation of pioneers who are willing to take risks to see the Kingdom come in every sphere of life. This book will serve as a handbook for many to take the steps needed to start activating a life of supernatural breakthrough. Filled with practical stories and nuggets of truth, this book will stir you into a life of Kingdom exploits, deeply motivated by love. Wendy's book will help you discover just how easy it is to live in the Kingdom of God. Read it and live it.'
Julian and Katia Adams, Founders of Frequentsee Trust, a prophetic ministry equipping churches and organisations with a Kingdom and reformation culture.

'I am very happy to commend Wendy Mann's book Naturally Supernatural. The book is full of grace, encourages us to believe in the power of God to heal today and contains helpful practical encouragement to us to step out and trust God. The book is realistic in terms of what happens when our prayers are not fully answered without in any way diminishing our determination to step out in faith to see God's miracle-working power today. Wendy's warm personality and testimonies of her own life serve to enhance the book's message.'

David Devenish, international church planter, leader of the Catalyst Network of Churches within Newfrontiers and author of *Demolishing Strongholds* (Authentic, 2013), *Fathering Leaders, Motivating Mission* (Authentic, 2011) and *What on Earth is the Church For?* (Wipf & Stock Publishers, 2005).

I was in a coffee shop with my daughter when I recognised Wendy at the table next to me. I started a conversation with her, explaining that I saw her when I visited King's Arms [church] on Mother's Day. I was a Jehovah's Witness, but having doubts about my faith.

I introduced my daughter who was in an emotionally troubled state, especially struggling at night. I was very conscious of scratches on her arm but Wendy did not make any reference to them, instead she looked at her and asked if she was having trouble sleeping. My daughter said she was and then let Wendy pray for her. I was overwhelmed by Wendy's kindness and the way she showed such love to my daughter. After praying, Wendy turned to me and asked if I was creative and if I made cards. I told her I did and she told me that God loved my creativity.

I was deeply impacted by the way Wendy prayed. It was like she really knew Jesus. I had been a Jehovah's Witness for twenty-two years but had never prayed like that because it did not come out of relationship. When we left the coffee shop, Wendy encouraged me to find her when I next visited King's Arms.

A week later, a couple from the church invited me to their small group to pray for my daughter. That night I decided to give my life to Jesus, and the following Sunday I went to church and found Wendy to tell her the news. Since that time, both my daughter and my grandson have also given their lives to Jesus and we love being part of King's Arms.

Ann: Coffee shop in Bedford

I always considered myself a Christian, but when I moved to the UK from South Africa I became detached from God. I stopped praying unless I was in need of something and never even considered attending church.

Eight years later, I started cutting the hair of a lady called Claire. I was a mobile hairdresser so went to her house fairly regularly. One day, Claire told me about a picture God had given her for me about my faith. She described it as being like embers of fire, not quite dead but something that could be reignited.

During another visit, I was suffering with an extremely painful left wrist. It had been painful for about four months and I was scared because my hands were my livelihood. Claire could see I was struggling and asked if she could pray for me. I was more than willing and quite intrigued. She placed her hand on my wrist and prayed that God would heal me. Almost as soon as she said amen the pain had gone! As the days and months went past, and my pain did not return, I humbly accepted that I had experienced a miracle.

Those embers Claire had a picture of have now been reignited. My time with Claire and her husband, Tony, have reminded me of God's amazing love and grace. I want to keep experiencing these things until the day I meet Him.
Carla: Client's house in Hove

A few months ago I was sitting in a coffee shop, totally immersed in work. I was going through a period of immense stress and pressure. Not only were my publishing company reminding me that the manuscript of a book I was writing on leadership had to be submitted that day, it was also the day a buyer for my company was pushing for a decision – sell to them now, or walk away from the deal altogether.

In a state of confusion and utter despair, my thoughts were interrupted by a female voice: 'Hi, my friends who are sitting over there and I had a strong sense from God to give you this message.' This smiling lady eagerly handed me a note. She continued, 'If you'd like to read it and it makes sense, feel free to come and join us and we can pray for you.'

I opened the note and started to read: 'We see leadership within you...' The note continued to talk about my leadership calling (this was the book I was writing) and ended with 'God knows that you're under enormous pressure to make a decision about your work right now, but fear not about financial pressure as God wants to let you know that He will provide – follow your path and go with your heart.'

There was no way that these lovely folk could have known about the pressures I was under that day, yet every word they wrote had profound congruency with what was happening in my life. Realising that God was watching over me, I went over to their table and we prayed. I got the book in and I made the right decision about the business sale.

The next day I went to watch these ladies graduate from TSM [Training for Supernatural Ministry] at King's Arms Church. I felt an amazing spirit at the church and I am still going along. Ever since that day I have felt God much closer, guiding me and illuminating the right path ahead.

Anthony: Coffee shop in Bedford

CONTENTS

ACKNOWLEDGEMENTS

There are so many I want to thank who have helped me on the journey of writing this book.

Mum and Dad, thank you for your unconditional love. You constantly cheer me on as I have new adventures with God. I am so grateful for the way you believe in me.

Simon and PJ, thank you for encouraging me to step in to leadership way before I was ready! Thank you for trusting me with TSM. I am so grateful to serve such an incredible team of Elders who are so releasing and passionate about me being me.

TSM team past and present, thank you for giving yourselves wholeheartedly to see many believers trained and equipped to live naturally supernatural lives. You have taught me so much about having fun on the journey.

TSM students, thank you for your hunger for more of God. Thank you for the price you have paid to see God's Kingdom break in with increasing momentum. I love our family!

Ali, thank you for being an amazing friend. You have consistently championed me in my writing adventure. Thank you for spending hours reading and rereading chapters. This book is better because of you.

Claire, Ruth and Rah, thank you for your friendship and encouragement. The truth you have spoken has helped me to really believe in this book.

Toby, thank you for your creativity and patience.

Heavenly Father, without You there is no book! Thank You for giving me such an incredible race to run.

FOREWORD

Wendy Mann is an inspiring lady. I have watched her over many years pursue God through good times and tough times with a relentless energy. When at the King's Arms we were seeing very little supernatural breakthrough, Wendy was one who stood with me to ask God for more. She stepped out time and again in simple obedience to God's command to 'heal the sick and preach the gospel'. It was watching her grow in gifting and confidence that inspired so many in the church to follow her example and ask God for His power. Seeing many people healed and many others come into freedom became expected around Wendy, and I loved it when she came to me with another story of breakthrough; it never ceased to excite her.

When she herself became ill, it was watching her walk through the pain, disappointment and uncertainty of her own condition that led many to realise that this was a woman who depended on God whatever the circumstances. Her determination to walk it through closely with her Father was a wonderful example of the grace of God. Wendy didn't hesitate to share authentically the challenges of her situation, but she maintained a strong faith throughout that her Father was good and He would see her through!

One hallmark of Wendy sets her apart from others with a ministry of signs and wonders; her passion for raising up others and seeing them walk in the freedom in God that she herself has discovered. Wendy is not content to keep it to herself and she loves giving away all that God has given her to see a multiplication of God's power and life in the church. Many have moved from hopelessness and passivity as they have come under her influence, and have become passionate sons and daughters, taking the Kingdom of God wherever they go. She inspires a childlike faith in those who hear her and in this, her first written adventure, I know that you will catch that same spirit.

Prepare to be challenged, provoked, inspired and moved as you read Wendy's story and hear the things that she has learnt and wants to pass on to you. Don't rush this book but instead take your time. These are lessons from a battle-hardened warrior that will build you up and strengthen you as you fight your own fight to see the kingdom of darkness pushed back and people come into freedom all around you. Wendy is a true hero of the faith and I count it a privilege to be her friend and co-worker. I hope you enjoy getting to know her better through these pages.

Simon Holley
Senior Leader, King's Arms Church

1
THE NORMAL CHRISTIAN LIFE

In my first year at university I got invited by a friend to do an Alpha course at King's Arms Church in Bedford.[1] I had been brought up going to church and would have said that I was a Christian. It felt a bit awkward doing a course that was meant to introduce me to Jesus. I had no idea that one particular evening would have such a profound impact on the trajectory of my life.

The talk was entitled, 'Does God heal today?' Towards the end of the evening, the course leader stood up and announced that he wanted to demonstrate practically how to pray for the sick. He asked if anyone in the room had pain in one of their ears, explaining that God had told him about it earlier in the day. I remember feeling relieved that it was not me. I did not know what was about to happen, but I was keen not to suddenly become the centre of attention. I looked around the room to see if what God had 'told the leader' was relevant to anyone. To my surprise, a young man raised his hand. The course leader invited this guy to stand at the front of the room to be prayed for, and we were encouraged to watch what God would do. I remember staring at the man, having no idea what was about to happen. The course leader put his hand on this guy's ear, said a very short and simple prayer, and then asked him how his ear was doing. The man seemed confused and unsure of how to respond as he raised his hand to touch his ear. He told us that all the pain had gone! It was the first time I saw someone healed in front of my eyes.

On the same evening, a small team came from the church to prophesy over us. I did not know what prophecy was. I remember a lady I had never seen before picking me out to share what she felt God wanted to say to me. She talked about there being a hunger in my heart for more of God and to know Him personally. The way she phrased her sentences made it feel like she had been reading my mind. God showed me in that moment how intimately He knew me and loved me. These two experiences woke something up in me. God put something in my spirit that convinced me that what I had seen and experienced should be the normal Christian life for me and for every believer.

I was studying to be a sports teacher at the time, so there were no shortage of opportunities to pray for the sick, as so many of my peers had sporting injuries. The only problem was that I had immense amounts of fear. When I say immense amounts I am not exaggerating. I remember once as a child having to find out people's favourite sandwich fillings for a school project, but being too shy even to ask a man fitting tiles in our bathroom. My mum had to ask him for me! The thought of offering to pray for my injured friends at university petrified me, but I could not shake the conviction God had put in me. I was convinced that seeing the sick healed was meant to be a regular occurrence for every believer, even the introverts like me.

I will never forget the first time I prayed for someone and

saw them healed. I was walking home from a lecture with a friend who started to complain about pain in her knee. I told my friend God loves to heal and asked if I could pray for her. She was happy for me to do so. It did not occur to me that I could have prayed for her right there on the street, so I invited her back to my house.

When we got home I simply copied what I had seen the Alpha course leader do a few weeks earlier. I put my hand on my friend's knee and said a very short and simple prayer. When I asked how her knee was she told me that nothing had changed. I apologised that my prayer had not worked and she left to go home. I did not know I could have prayed more than once. I had only seen one person healed, and they had been healed instantly!

Later that day, there was a knock at the door. It was my friend with her housemate, and my friend was grinning from ear to ear. She told me that when she got home the pain in her knee suddenly got really intense and then it completely disappeared. God had healed her knee and it happened as a result of my prayer. She told me that her housemate had been playing cricket all day and had badly injured his thumb, and they were wondering if I could do anything about it! I prayed for her housemate's thumb and he left about 90 per cent healed. I spent the evening replaying what had happened in my mind. God had used my prayers to heal people! It took me a while to recover from the adrenaline rush of pushing through so much fear. I was shocked by all that had happened, but felt more alive than ever. I had tasted what the normal Christian life could be like and I did not want to go back.

I am assuming because you are reading this book that you too have a desire to see God's Kingdom come in your everyday life; to see your prayers impact the lives of those around you so that Jesus is made famous on the earth. The aim of the rest of this book is to share some of what I have learnt over the years as I have intentionally pursued a naturally supernatural life. There have been many challenges along the way, but also great joys and many miracles. My hope is that through reading this book you will feel empowered and equipped to live the normal Christian life.

FOLLOWING JESUS' EXAMPLE

The best way to know what the normal Christian life can look like is to look at how Jesus lived His life. When Peter, Jesus' disciple, is asked to tell a group of Gentiles everything he had been commanded by the Lord, he summarises Jesus' life like this: 'God anointed Jesus of Nazareth with the Holy Spirit and power … he went around doing good and healing all who were under the power of the devil, because God was with him' (Acts 10:38, NIV UK 2011). I love this! I believe what Peter describes here is meant to be the normal Christian life for every believer.

You only have to skim-read the Gospels to realise that Jesus' major focus was on proclaiming and demonstrating the Kingdom, the rule and reign of God, wherever He went. Everywhere Jesus went, the Kingdom broke in: people were healed and some even got raised from the dead, people got set free from spiritual oppression and brought back into community, words of knowledge opened people's hearts, food was multiplied and a storm was calmed. Many people's lives were radically transformed as Jesus went about His everyday life, proclaiming and demonstrating the Kingdom of God.

It was never Jesus' intention that He would be the only one

to live this way. While His disciples were still very much in training, Jesus sent them out to do the things they had seen Him do. Jesus told His disciples, 'The harvest is plentiful, but the labourers are few; therefore pray earnestly to the Lord of the harvest to send out labourers into his harvest' (Matthew 9:37,38). The number of people ready to hear about and encounter God's Kingdom was vast, but the number of people sharing it was too few. Jesus urged His disciples to pray for more people to be mobilised to talk about and demonstrate the Kingdom. Almost immediately the disciples became the answer to their own prayers.

Jesus gathered His disciples and gave them authority over unclean spirits and to heal every disease and affliction. Then He sent them out with the following instruction, 'go … to the lost sheep of the house of Israel. And proclaim as you go, saying, "The kingdom of heaven is at hand." Heal the sick, raise the dead, cleanse lepers, cast out demons. You received without paying; give without pay' (Matthew 10:6–8). The disciples got drafted in to Jesus' mission to see the rule and reign of God break out all over the planet. Jesus' intention was to model what was possible for every believer and then train, equip and release His disciples to do what He had been doing.

When Jesus ascended into heaven, His desire to see the Kingdom break in did not diminish. On the day of Pentecost, all Jesus' disciples who were gathered in Jerusalem were powerfully anointed with the Holy Spirit to live this life that Jesus had modelled (Acts 2). When the Holy Spirit came, the church was born and the disciples saw powerful demonstrations of God's Kingdom wherever they went.

It is still Jesus' desire to see the Kingdom of God advance on the earth. The kingdom of the enemy brings brokenness, destruction, sickness and death. The Kingdom of God brings life, healing, freedom and wholeness. Jesus is passionate about His Father's Kingdom overpowering and defeating the enemy's schemes, and it is still His plan to see the Kingdom come through His disciples. 'His disciples' means any of us who follow Him. Of course, it is God who saves and heals and it is God who sets people free and transforms people's lives. There is no pressure on us to have to make something happen, and yet, Jesus wants us to co-labour with Him.

Anyone who thinks that being a Christian is boring has not understood the incredible adventure we have been invited in to!

A friend of mine was asked to go to a community group in her church to teach them about healing the sick. The group consisted of people who were mostly over sixty. As part of her training, my friend encouraged the group to look for opportunities to pray for people who were sick the following week. She advised them to have a story of healing ready to share with anyone they might meet to help build their faith.

She met with the group on a Tuesday, and the following Sunday one of the ladies who was eighty-five approached her excitedly. She had done it! She had approached an elderly man in her village who she often chatted to who suffered with a bad back and bad leg. She had told him about stories she had heard of God healing people and had asked if she could pray for him. The man agreed and seemed very touched by the offer. Over the course of the conversation, this adventurous lady also got to tell the man that God loved him. This 85-year-old kingdom-bringer was almost ready to burst with joy when she told my friend how she had taken this opportunity to see God's Kingdom come.

I love this story and it saddens me all at the same time. I love it because a lady in her eighties offered to pray for someone on the streets for the very first time.[2] I love it because it teaches us that you are never too old to start pursuing a naturally supernatural life. I love it because of how excited the lady got when she realised God wanted to use her in the same way that He wants to use all of us.

But it saddens me too. It saddens me that this lady had to wait until she was eighty-five to be equipped and empowered to see God's Kingdom break out. It saddens me to think about how she might have been used by God if she had been encouraged to go for it when she was sixty, or thirty, or even twelve. It saddens me because this is not unusual: I am realising that there are many Christians around the world who do not know they are called and equipped to see God's Kingdom break out wherever they go. I dream of that changing. I want every believer to know that a naturally supernatural life is meant to be the norm for them. I want to see every believer in every church mobilised to see Jesus glorified on the earth.

I like to imagine what churches would look like if every believer realised that the life Jesus modelled is possible for them too. To be 'anointed with the Holy Spirit and power, to go around doing good, to heal all under the power of the devil because God is with them'. What would the villages or towns or cities that had these kind of believers in look like? I think in the past we have relied too heavily on 'men and women of power' to see the Kingdom break in. It is true that God anoints certain people to pioneer breakthrough in signs and wonders and demonstrations of God's power, but their lives are meant to be an inspiration to us to ask God for more. Every Christian is called to do the things that Jesus did: to see God's Kingdom break out wherever they go.

To help us as we go, I think there are four lessons we can learn about the normal Christian life from Peter's summary of Jesus.

JESUS WAS ANOINTED WITH THE HOLY SPIRIT AND POWER

Jesus was anointed with the Holy Spirit right at the beginning of His ministry. After He was baptised, the Holy Spirit descended on Him like a dove and His Father affirmed Him from heaven, 'You are my beloved Son; with you I am well pleased' (Mark 1:11). Jesus modelled throughout His ministry the dual importance of knowing God as His Father and also knowing the truth of His identity as a dearly loved son. These two things equipped Him with power to see the Kingdom of God break out wherever He went. It is these two things that will equip us too.

It is the Holy Spirit who gives us revelation of who God is as our Father. He also reveals to us that we are God's beloved sons and daughters: 'For you did not receive the spirit of slavery to fall back into fear, but you have received the Spirit of adoption as sons, by whom we cry, "Abba! Father!" The Spirit himself bears witness with our spirit that we are children of God' (Romans 8:15,16). When you know who God is as your Father, and you know who you are as His dearly loved child, it changes everything.

One of the reasons we are passionate at TSM about prioritising God's presence is the Holy Spirit's role in bringing this revelation to our hearts.[3] When God's presence comes, people receive a greater revelation of who He is and how much He loves them. They also get revelation of their identity in Christ and of who they are as His dearly loved children. This revelation of God's love for us causes the love we feel for those around us to go to a whole new level. And the revelation of our true identity in Christ gives us confidence to believe that we are anointed to bring breakthrough where God's Kingdom has not yet come. This revelation propels us on the journey of learning to live like Jesus.

One of our TSM students wrestled for a long time with his identity. He struggled to understand that he was a beloved son of God and what that even meant. He would often compare himself to other people on the course and end up feeling like he did not really fit. Then one morning at TSM, he shared that he had experienced breakthrough. The Holy Spirit had spoken to him very personally and given him deep revelation of his identity as God's son.

Later in the year, this same student shared about an encounter he had one weekend when he was collecting a piece of second-hand furniture his wife had bought online. He had to travel quite a distance to pick it up and was feeling a bit frustrated about the journey, but the Holy Spirit whispered to him that this was an opportunity, not a problem. The student began to ask God for an opportunity to show His love to the lady he was getting the furniture from (sons do that kind of thing). He felt God prompt him to offer to pray for a pancreatic condition.

When he got to the lady's house and had loaded the furniture into his car, he had to fight the urge to retreat as quickly as possible without mentioning that God had spoken to him. After some hesitation the student made a courageous choice to walk through fear and ask the lady if she had anything wrong with her pancreas. The lady seemed quite taken aback. She explained that she had been having pain in her abdomen for a while but had been too scared to go to the doctor to get it checked, even though her husband had encouraged her to. After more conversation, the student had the opportunity to pray for this bewildered lady and tell her that God had spoken about her situation because He loved her.

When the student returned home, he had an email waiting for him from his newfound friend. The furniture lady had lots of questions about what had happened. She wanted to know if the student was actually a psychic, because how else could he have known about her situation? The student emailed back to explain more about Jesus and how He sometimes speaks through words of knowledge. After a couple more emails back and forth, the lady acknowledged that the student must have been sent to her for a reason. She told the student she would make an appointment to see the doctor and she thanked him for being so kind and caring. To say that the encounter impacted her is an understatement.[4]

The revelation this student had about his identity, about who he really is as God's beloved son, caused him to start expecting to see God's Kingdom come in his everyday life. The truth is that all of us, like Jesus, are anointed with the Holy Spirit and with power. We are called and commissioned to see God's Kingdom come wherever we go, even when doing something as normal as collecting furniture we have bought online.

HE WENT AROUND DOING GOOD

I love that a key part of Peter's summary of Jesus' life is that He went around doing good. It makes following Jesus' example so accessible for all of us. We can often over-complicate what it looks like to live a naturally supernatural life. The truth is that it is as simple as going around doing good. The key is to have a foundation of love in our hearts for the people God puts in front of us. When our default position is to demonstrate God's love to someone, we realise that encouraging someone or giving them a gift or helping them practically is just as much the Kingdom breaking in as praying for healing or giving the gospel.

I remember when a small group in our church decided to buy some chocolate and a thank you card for a traffic warden. They wanted to thank her for doing a good job in our town and bless her with a very simple gift. This traffic warden did not know what to do with the encouragement. She told the group that earlier in the day someone had tried to run over her foot, that someone else had told her they wished she had cancer, and that someone else had spat at her as she tried to do her job. The encouragement and gift from the group spoke volumes to this lady. God's Kingdom broke in because God's heart was demonstrated through this very simple act of the church going around doing good.

On another occasion, one of our TSM outreach teams wanted to thank people who had to be outside in the rain because of their job. In the pouring rain, they took a cup of coffee and some cake to a man who was in charge of security for a car park in the town. He had to sit in a small wooden hut by himself day in and day out. They went up to the man and explained that they wanted to thank him for all he was doing. The guy seemed completely stunned. He told the team that he had been doing the same job for eleven years but that he had never been thanked before. God's Kingdom broke in through encouragement and honour that day. The words we speak have such incredible power.

What amazes me about God is that when we choose to

really love and value people without a hidden agenda, He often opens up opportunities for His Kingdom to break in supernaturally as well. I remember walking through Bedford town centre with a friend, looking for people to encourage. We spotted a guy who was in charge of cleaning toilets so we decided to go over and thank him for doing such a great job. He seemed really encouraged by what we said and told us he had been cleaning the same toilets for twenty years!

We spoke together for quite a while, and then out of the blue this man started telling us about a dream he had had. As he shared the dream, I felt God begin to give me the interpretation. This had never happened to me before, so I was keen to share what I felt God was saying. The man was intrigued by what I said and agreed that it made some sense to him. He then went on to tell us about his estranged daughter who he had recently got back in touch with, and we were able to encourage him about being a father. Over the course of our time together, we got to pray for this precious man twice and demonstrate God's love to him. As a result of our intention to honour and encourage this man, God opened up a supernatural encounter.

Another time, a TSM team was giving out cakes to people they met on the streets near to our church building. When they offered a cake to one particular passer-by he refused, explaining he was not allowed to eat wheat or dairy. He lifted up his shirt to reveal a large scar on his abdomen and explained that he had bowel cancer that was spreading. Our team had the privilege of asking him how he was doing emotionally, and then praying for him for complete healing. They also got to encourage him for being so courageous. A supernatural opportunity opened up because they were giving away free cakes in the community. As we go about doing good, with love as our foundation and no hidden agenda, God opens up exciting opportunities to see His Kingdom break in. It really is that easy.

HEALING ALL WHO WERE UNDER THE POWER OF THE DEVIL

Anyone who has not yet given their life to Jesus is under the influence of the enemy, and anywhere you see the opposite of the Kingdom of God, the 'power of the devil' is at work. It is important that out of our foundation of loving the people God puts in front of us we also expect to see supernatural breakthrough in their lives. If we meet someone who has cancer, we love them by encouraging them and helping them practically where they need it. We also love them by praying for a miracle in their body. If we meet someone who is really struggling in their marriage, we love them by spending time with them and listening to how they are doing. We also love them by praying for supernatural breakthrough so that their marriage is restored. Both the practical support and prayer for supernatural breakthrough come out of the love God puts in our hearts for the person in front of us.

To follow Jesus means to have an appetite for the impossible, to live with a passion to see the supernatural power of God break in to transform impossible situations. To follow Jesus means to live with a conviction that there are no dead-end or hopeless cases. We are commissioned by God to powerfully advance His Kingdom on the earth. The same Holy Spirit who anointed Jesus with power is available for every believer. It is such a privilege to be used by God to see those living under the oppression and influence of the enemy encounter freedom and fullness of life as God's power breaks in.

I was on my way to a church meeting once and God

opened up a two-hour encounter with three teenagers. It came about out of nothing. I walked past one of them and said hello and somehow we got talking. A friend and I ended up prophesying over the three of them, and one of the girls started to cry as God spoke directly into her situation. God then spoke to me about one of them having a bad back. The slightly inebriated teenage boy said it was him. I asked if he had one leg shorter than the other, but he was not sure so I asked him to sit down on the pavement with his back against a wall. One of his legs was about an inch shorter than the other. Suddenly feeling more confident, I encouraged the two girls to gather round as I prayed to see what God would do. After a couple of short prayers, the boy's leg grew out and all the pain in his back had gone!

I wish you could have seen the look on those teenagers' faces. One of their friends had just encountered the supernatural power of a God they did not believe in. Over the course of the next hour, the two girls also experienced physical healing and my friend and I got to answer some of their questions about God. When it was time for us to go, we hugged goodbye as if we had known each other for years. None of the teenagers got saved that night, but each of them encountered Jesus' love and kindness and moved a step closer to Him. My friend and I missed our meeting, but we both commented on how alive we felt, seeing God's Kingdom come on the streets. This was what we had been made for.

When people experience the supernatural power of God they encounter His kindness, and Scripture teaches us that it is the kindness of God that leads to repentance (Romans 2:4). A friend of mine was on the phone with her ex-boss. She had spoken to him a lot about Jesus over the years. He was quite open spiritually and believed in a universal energy, but that is as far as it went. My friend had recently heard a talk I had done about how God gets our attention if He wants us to pray for people. One of the examples I had used was when people start to speak to us out of the blue about their sickness or an injury they have.

As my friend was speaking to her ex-boss, he began to tell her about a fall he had had and that he was in a lot of pain in his knees. My friend realised God was setting her up. She explained that she could pray for him over the phone if he was up for it, and he was. She encouraged him to put his hands on his knees and as he did so she commanded healing to come. When she asked what was happening, her ex-boss explained that his knees had got really hot. My friend encouraged him to walk around and do something he could not do before. After the first time of praying, the pain in one of his knees had gone; after the second time, the pain in both knees had gone; after the third time, pain he had in other parts of his body as a result of the fall had totally disappeared. God's Kingdom broke in and this man encountered the love of Jesus as his body was healed. The Sunday after this happened, he came to church for the first time in forty years and responded by giving his life to Jesus!

Whatever the outcome of an encounter, being a disciple of Jesus involves showing the world powerful demonstrations of God's Kingdom. It involves living with the conviction that we are called to see the domain of the enemy infiltrated and overcome by the rule and reign of Christ. We must not settle for anything less than regular supernatural breakthrough as we follow Jesus and seek to represent Him to the world around us. How are you doing at having an appetite for the impossible?

BECAUSE GOD WAS WITH HIM

What a brilliant way for Peter to end his summary. Jesus did all that He did because God was with Him. Simple as that! At the end of Jesus' commission to His disciples He makes this profound statement: 'And behold, I am with you always, to the end of the age' (Matthew 28:20). This promise is from the King of the universe, the one who has defeated death and is in charge of everything. He is the one who sits in the heavens and laughs at the days to come because nothing can get in the way of His plans. He is the one who has all power and authority and all things under His feet. This God promises to always be with us. This God is stretching out His hand to heal and perform signs and wonders (Acts 4:30). This God has our backs!

Jesus is always with us through the Holy Spirit, who anoints us and fills us. I am making an assumption that you understand what it means to be filled with the Holy Spirit. I will not go into more detail here, but if baptism in the Holy Spirit is a new concept to you, I would encourage you to spend some time looking into it. Being filled with the Holy Spirit changes everything.[5]

God, who is always with us and now dwells in us, is much more passionate about His Kingdom breaking in than we will ever be. He is the only one who can save and heal and set people free. This takes the pressure off us and makes sharing God's love with people a joy and a privilege rather than something heavy and stressful. Jesus is in charge. His Kingdom is forcefully advancing and always increasing. We get to go along for the ride and see many people's lives transformed on the journey.

As Peter is still telling the group of Gentiles all that Jesus had told him, something exciting takes place. 'While Peter was still saying these things, the Holy Spirit fell on all who heard the word. And the believers from among the circumcised who had come with Peter were amazed, because the gift of the Holy Spirit was poured out even on the Gentiles' (Acts 10:44,45). The Jews believed that the Gentiles were outside the purposes of God, but God speaks loud and clear here. The same Holy Spirit who had anointed Jesus to do what He did, and the same Holy Spirit who had anointed the disciples at Pentecost was now anointing the Gentiles. The life that Jesus lived was not just to be replicated by the Jews. It was to be the normal Christian life for every believer.

If you want to go up a level in really grasping this truth, spend some time dreaming with God about seeing His Kingdom break in. Think about where you would like to be used by God and who you would like God to meet with. The aim of the rest of this book is to help you put your dreams into practice and equip you to live a naturally supernatural life so that Jesus is increasingly glorified on the earth. Wherever you are on your journey, let this truth get hold of your heart: 'All things are possible for one who believes' (Mark 9:23).

NOTES

1. King's Arms is my home church where I have walked out this journey of pursuing the normal Christian life. For more information go to: www.kingsarms.org

2. When I use the phrase 'on the streets' I am referring to any breakthrough that happens outside of organised church meetings. 'On the streets' encounters do not always take place literally on a street.

3. TSM stands for Training for Supernatural Ministry. It is a nine-month training school designed to equip believers to live a naturally supernatural life. For more details go to www.kingsarms.org/tsm

4. Often when I use the term 'encounter' I am talking about an opportunity

God opens up for His Kingdom to advance through us.

5. For more information about being filled with the Holy Spirit, watch 'Changed by the Spirit' by Simon Holley, http://www.kingsarms.org/resources/media/message/changed-by-the-spirit.html, or read Nicky Gumbel, *Questions of Life: Alpha Course* (London: Alpha International Publications, 2010).

2
KNOW WHO
GOD IS

Several years ago, I had the privilege of spending a week in Redding, California. I went on a trip to visit Bethel church and had an amazing time encountering God and getting refreshed and re-envisioned.[1] The main thing that struck me while I was there was the powerful corporate expectation that God was going to be good. When you walked into the church it was clear that people did not just believe God was generally good, they actually expected Him to be good to them. It had such a profound impact on me because I knew I was not living with the same expectation. The teaching I heard did not deny that bad and painful things happen, and I was very aware of people really loving each other and standing with one another through difficult times. What was unique to me was the fact that even though difficult circumstances needed to be walked through, it did not seem to shake people's foundational belief in a good God and their expectation of His goodness. Unsurprisingly, the corporate expectation of good things from God resulted in exceptional fruit.

In order to live a naturally supernatural life, it is so important to have revelation in our hearts about the true nature of God, about who He is and what He is like. This is different to knowing who God is in your head. It is important to really know in the depths of your being that the God you follow is first and foremost a God of love. It is important to know that He is good and cannot be anything but good. Revelation that He is Healer and Saviour and that He is zealous about His Kingdom breaking out all over the planet is crucial. Knowing this truth in your head alone will not be enough. One of the main ways the enemy stops us living what I believe should be the normal Christian life is by lying to us about the nature of God, about who God is. Without revelation of the truth that impacts our hearts we will be more susceptible to believing those lies, and our effectiveness in seeing God's Kingdom come will be limited.

I remember God speaking to me about the importance of this revelation when I spent time with Him in my room one evening. I had been reading books full of stories about ordinary men and women who had done major exploits for God, seeing His Kingdom break out in mind-blowing ways. I knew I was called and equipped, just like the people I read about, to see the same things happen, and I knew God was eager to use me. At the same time, I was becoming increasingly aware of lies I believed that were holding me back; lies about not having enough faith to see the miraculous, that God was more likely to use other people than me, and that I had too much fear in my life to approach strangers on the streets. I knew I had to get better at ignoring lies and believing the truth, and God seemed to underline the importance of this as I read some verses in Matthew's Gospel that evening.

Matthew 16 tells us that Jesus asked His disciples who people said He was. He then asked them the same question. 'Now when Jesus came into the district of Caesarea Philippi, he asked his disciples, "Who do people say that the Son of Man is?" And they said, "Some say John the Baptist, others say Elijah, and others Jeremiah or one of the prophets." He said to them, "But who do you say that I am?" Simon Peter replied, "You are the Christ, the Son of the living God." And Jesus answered him, "Blessed are you, Simon Bar-Jonah! For flesh and blood has not revealed this to you, but my Father who is in heaven. And I tell you, you are Peter, and on this rock I will build my church, and the gates of hell shall not prevail against it"' (Matthew 16:13–18).

Simon Peter piped up with the right answer. 'You are the Christ, the son of the living God.' Jesus' response shows us that Simon Peter knew this as a result of direct revelation from the Father. This was not just head knowledge for Simon Peter; God had revealed the true nature of Jesus to Him in his heart.

I now know that there is much discussion in commentaries about the rock Jesus references in this passage. Some say that Peter was the rock the church would be built on. Peter was in charge of establishing the first church after Pentecost (Acts 2) and he was the first apostle to extend the gospel to the Gentiles (Acts 10). Some say that Jesus was referring to Himself as the rock the church would be built on. Others argue that the rock was to do with the revelation Peter received, that the rock the church would be built on was revelation. I was unaware of any of these discussions as I was reading the scripture that evening. As I prayed, I felt God draw my attention to the revelation Peter received. God spoke to me about the church being built on the rock of revelation.[2]

God highlighted two key areas of revelation Peter received in his encounter with Jesus. Firstly he received revelation of who Jesus was, and because of that, revelation of the true nature of God. When you understand who Jesus is, you understand the Father. As the writer to the Hebrews explains, 'He [Jesus] is the radiance of the glory of God and the exact imprint of his nature' (Hebrews 1:3). Secondly, Peter received revelation of who Jesus said he was: 'And I tell you, you are Peter' (Matthew 16:18). I felt like God gave me two huge keys in the pursuit of a naturally supernatural life that night: really know who God is, and really know who He says you are; in other words, your brand new identity in Christ. I believe this revelation is crucial if the church is to be built on strong foundations, and the enemy knows it.

THE BATTLE IS IN THE MIND

The battle for this revelation is fought primarily in the mind. I realised as I looked into this more closely that the lies the enemy feeds us can be separated broadly into these two main categories. Firstly, lies about who God is: His nature, His character and His heart. Secondly, lies about who God says we are: our identity in Christ. As believers, it is important that we train ourselves to identify and ignore the lies and choose instead to believe the truth about who God is and who He says we are. This will put us in a very powerful position when it comes to being used by God to see His Kingdom break in. The next chapter will focus on the battle for our identity, but in this chapter we will unpack how we position ourselves for greater revelation of the true nature of God.

The enemy loves it when Christians believe lies about who God is and what He is like. It was a key tactic he used right at the beginning of the story, when Adam and Eve were in the Garden of Eden. God told Adam and Eve they could eat from every tree in the garden, except for the tree of the knowledge of good and evil. If they were to eat of that tree, God warned them that there would be devastating consequences. Adam and Eve had so much freedom in the garden, and there was only one restriction, which was in place for their own good. The enemy got Adam and Eve to disobey God and eat from the tree that was out of bounds by calling into question God's heart, specifically His goodness:

'But the serpent said to the woman, "You will not surely die. For God knows that when you eat of it your eyes will be opened, and you will be like God, knowing good and evil"' (Genesis 3:4,5).

The enemy questioned God's goodness by suggesting to Eve that He was withholding something good from her and Adam. The enemy lied about the nature of God and the motive of His heart, and Eve fell for it. The rest is history.

This is still a favourite tactic of the enemy and his demonic spirits. If they can get us to believe lies about the nature and character of God, then they know that our relationship with Him will become fractured. If they can get us to doubt God's goodness or question His motives, then they know that our ability to trust God will be limited. When the enemy and his workforce succeed in getting us to agree with lies about who God is, they know it makes us ineffective in seeing God's Kingdom break out wherever we go. For example, it is difficult to expect God to heal someone you meet on the streets if you are having doubts about His willingness to heal.

The enemy feeds us lies about who God is by making us focus on our circumstances. 'God does not provide because I am trapped in financial debt'; 'God does not love to heal because I have prayed so many times for breakthrough but I am still sick'; 'God is not good because He did not intervene when my friend was dying'; 'God does not love me or my spouse because our marriage is falling apart'; 'God is not kind because I did not get the job I really wanted and I was the most qualified for the position'… The lies go on and on. What lies are you being told?

Our agreement with the enemy's lies will attack our ability to trust in the unwavering goodness of God. This is turn will impact our expectation when it comes to seeing signs and wonders as part of our everyday lives. If you struggle to believe God is good, you will struggle to believe that He wants to be good to the person you have just met on the street, or your work colleague, or that family member. The truth is, God is perfect in every way and His nature never changes. It is vital that we learn to recognise lies from the enemy, or wrong thinking we have about God as a result of our past experiences, so that we can ignore these and position ourselves for increased revelation of God's goodness. One of the ways we do that is by rooting out disappointment from our lives.

FAITH = BELIEF + EXPECTATION

Not long after my trip to Bethel, I was in a prayer meeting before church and God spoke to me very clearly about why I struggled to expect His goodness in my life like I had witnessed there. 'Your problem, Wendy, is that rather than expecting my goodness, you are often expecting to be disappointed.' I was nailed! I realised that because I had experienced a lot of disappointment in my life up to that point, my heart was packed full of pain that stopped me being able to expect good things from God. I had never worked through my disappointment, and because it was still in my heart, my default was to expect to be disappointed again and again. My unprocessed disappointment was killing my faith.

I have heard faith defined as belief plus expectation. Believing God is good is different to actually expecting Him to be good to you. Believing He loves to heal is different to expecting Him to heal in the specific situation you are praying for. Unprocessed disappointment directly attacks our faith because it directly attacks our expectation. When we have disappointment in our hearts we will not expect too much from God 'just in case', because our primary concern is to protect ourselves from further disappointment and pain. We will also avoid promising others too much, 'just in case', because we do not want them to have to experience the pain of disappointment in their lives. Our disappointment causes us to guard our hearts and the hearts of those around us by lowering levels of expectation and, ultimately, faith. The problem with this is, if you do not expect very much from God, you are unlikely to experience very much.

I once heard someone say that the biggest barrier to spiritual breakthrough in the United Kingdom is disappointment in the heart of believers that has never been dealt with. I am inclined to agree, and I have experienced this to be true in other nations too. As I travel to different churches teaching people how to do the things that Jesus did, I come across so much unexpressed pain and disappointment in people's hearts. This leaves church communities struggling to stand in faith for God's Kingdom to break in. The answer to this disappointment epidemic in believers and the church is learning how to express and work through our disappointment in a healthy way. When we deal with disappointment, we are consistently able to come back to a place of faith in the goodness of God.

UNEXPECTED SICKNESS

In December 2006, I was diagnosed with having a large cyst on one of my ovaries. It was totally unexpected. There were no warning signs to suggest there was anything growing in my abdomen. After an initial consultation and blood test at my local hospital, I was informed that I would need to be transferred to Addenbrooke's Hospital in Cambridge for my treatment, as there was a risk that the cyst might be cancerous. Addenbrooke's had a specialist gynaecological oncology department, and I was quickly given an appointment with one of their surgeons to discuss my now imminent operation.

I had been praying for the sick to be healed at King's Arms for several years up to this point. My first experience of seeing someone healed at Alpha deposited a conviction in my heart that this was the normal Christian life, and I could expect to be used to see the sick healed inside and outside the church. We were praying for the sick every Sunday by this time and seeing some incredible breakthroughs, and I was expectant for more and more. Now it was my turn to experience miraculous intervention. I believed this was going to be my opportunity to be miraculously healed. The cyst would disappear as a result of prayer, I would grow in faith for the miraculous, and my friends and family who did not yet know Jesus would all come to know Him. It was only a matter of time and persevering in prayer.

Hundreds of people were praying for me both in the UK and other nations, but I never got the miraculous breakthrough I was longing for. My operation took place early in January 2007. I had to sign a consent form before I went in to surgery, giving the surgeon permission to give me a hysterectomy if he deemed it necessary after assessing the state of my womb and ovaries. I went for my operation with the very real possibility

I would wake up never being able to have children, and with the added possibility that I might need further treatment for cancer once I had had some time to recover.

To say that it was a difficult time is an understatement. Although there were many moments of God's kindness throughout the whole process, and I felt a supernatural peace on the morning of my operation, it was an exceptionally tough journey. I felt sick with fear when I thought about being in hospital and the possible outcome of my surgery, and I spent a lot of time crying with friends and God, confused as to why He had not intervened sooner to stop this happening.

The week I spent in hospital was very difficult, as were the first few weeks of recovery. I was in a lot of pain and I felt very ill. I also felt extremely lonely because I struggled to connect with God. The great news was that I came through the operation with my ovaries and womb completely intact, and after waiting two weeks to get the results of tests on the tumours, there was no trace of cancer. I was so grateful to God for His kindness and His clear intervention during the surgery to bring about the best outcome I could have hoped for. Yet despite the positive outcome, I realised my heart was still wracked with disappointment. I would often cry when I came into God's presence and think back to my time in hospital, remembering how hard it had been. I struggled generally to connect with God, it was difficult to trust Him to do good things in my life, and it was a challenge to believe Him for breakthrough when I prayed for other people.

As Christians, we can often jump from trauma we have experienced to the things we have to be thankful for in spite of difficult times, without properly dealing with the pain in between. I had hoped for a miracle, but as it turned out I had to have surgery. I am so grateful for the medical professionals who cared for me so well. I know that God uses doctors and surgeons and medicine to bring about healing, and I am so thankful for that. But I had hoped for supernatural breakthrough, and when I still needed surgery I was extremely disappointed. I could easily have chosen to just focus on the amazing outcome of my operation and not be real about the pain and disappointment of the journey. The truth is, it is important to focus on both the things that you are thankful for and the pain. Praying through my disappointment has enabled me to come back to a place of faith in God's desire and ability to heal. Understanding how to do this well is vitally important if you want to see God's Kingdom come on the earth.

DEALING WITH DISAPPOINTMENT

The first step on the journey of dealing with disappointment is realising that being real about your disappointment and expressing it to God is OK.[3] Many Christians believe the lie that to express pain they are struggling with to God, rather than focusing on what they have to be thankful for, means they are somehow dishonouring God and lacking faith. The truth is that until you get real with God about your disappointment you will struggle to really believe the truth about who He is, and it will be difficult to live with expectation in your heart. I love how David approaches God in Psalm 13: 'How long, O LORD? Will you forget me for ever? How long will you hide your face from me? How long must I take counsel in my soul and have sorrow in my heart all the day? How long shall my enemy be exalted over me?' (Psalm 13:1,2).

David is very honest with God. He does not hold back from

really telling God how he feels about what is going on, and he does not try to make things palatable because he is talking to the God of the universe. David gets real with his pain and what he is feeling. This is the second step in the process of dealing with disappointment. We need to get real with our emotions and connect with the pain in our hearts, holding nothing back.

The thing about dealing with disappointment is that it rarely happens by accident. Often it will take being intentional about blocking out time to be with God. I remember an evening I set aside to work through my disappointment with God from my operation. I shut myself away in my room and got real with God about the disappointment I felt about not being healed miraculously. There were loads of tears and a lot of snot as I expressed my pain to God about the whole operation process: 'When you didn't heal me, God, it felt like You didn't love me. When I was in the hospital, I felt so lonely it seemed like You had abandoned me. I don't understand why you didn't heal me. This was going to be my moment of breakthrough. I don't get it and I feel so disappointed.'

It is worth noting that I did not accuse God. I did not tell Him that He had abandoned me or that He did not love me or that He does not heal, because those statements are not true. Instead, I told God how I felt about what happened. When you express disappointment it is so important to be really honest with God without accusing Him. The truth is that He is perfect in every way and He never does anything wrong.

This expression of disappointment went on for a while until I felt like I came to the end of myself and I had said everything I needed to say. I decided to read the Psalms for a bit until I found one that expressed what I was feeling in my heart. Then in the place of having expressed all my pain to God, when I felt tired and vulnerable but strangely at peace in my heart, I began to declare the truth about who God is. I spoke out loud the truth about His heart and His character. This is the next step in dealing with disappointment. 'Thank You, God, that the truth is You are the Healer and You love to heal the sick. Thank You that the truth is You never leave me or forsake me; You were so close to me in the hospital. Thank You, God, that You love me with an everlasting love, You will never abandon me.' 'Death and life are in the power of the tongue' (Proverbs 18:21). Speaking the truth out loud rather than just thinking it is really important.

Being real about our disappointment gets all the pain clogging up our hearts and attacking our faith out of our system. When we then declare the truth about who God is, it goes really deep and our faith can be restored and strengthened. David models this process at the end of Psalm 13 when he comes back to the truth about who God is: 'But I have trusted in your steadfast love; my heart shall rejoice in your salvation. I will sing to the LORD, because he has dealt bountifully with me' (Psalm 13:5,6).

The last step in the journey of working through disappointment and so growing in revelation of the goodness of God is making a decision to lay down your right to understand.[4] Many of us believe that if we could just understand the hard things we go through, then we could know peace, yet the peace God promises is a peace that goes beyond our understanding. In his letter to the Philippians, Paul writes this: 'The Lord is at hand; do not be anxious about anything, but in everything by prayer and supplication with thanksgiving let your requests be made known to God. *And the peace of God, which surpasses all understanding,* will guard your heart and your minds in Christ Jesus' (Philippians 4:5–7, italics mine). Jesus is the Prince of Peace and He promises us a supernatural peace when we come to Him. The key for us is choosing to lay down our right to understand.

I remember praying for a friend who was pregnant with her second child. It was getting close to her due date and she was struggling with quite a bit of fear. She had been desperate for a normal delivery with her first baby, but complications had led to an emergency Caesarean section. She was carrying lots of disappointment about this, and was fearful that the same thing would happen again this time round. A friend and I went to pray for her. We led her through the process I have written about above, encouraging her to talk to God about how she felt when she had to be rushed into surgery. She was really courageous as she held nothing back, expressing her confusion and pain to God. There were lots of tears and lots of unanswered questions. The key moment during the prayer time came when we asked my friend if she felt able to give up her right to understand why things had not gone the way she had always dreamed they would go. She wrestled with more emotion for a bit, but then agreed to trust God with the things that still made no sense. She said, 'God, I lay down my right to understand why this happened and I choose to trust you.' I wish you could have been in the room at that moment. The supernatural peace of God rushed in, and my friend went from a place of fear to trust in her loving heavenly Father.

If we do not lay down our right to understand when tough things happen, not only will we miss out on the supernatural peace that is available to us, we will also run the risk of getting offended with God. Offence hardens our hearts and cuts us off from seeing God's Kingdom come in our lives. Jesus' interaction with John the Baptist recorded in Matthew 11 teaches us the importance of being quick to deal with offence that would want to infect our hearts. John sent his disciples to ask Jesus if He really was the Messiah. John had received revelation from God when he first saw Jesus that He was the one they had been waiting for (John 1:29), but now he was beginning to question that revelation. One of the first things John would have heard Jesus teach is that He had come to set the captives free, and yet John was stuck in prison. John's circumstance seemed to contradict who Jesus said He was, and John was on the verge of getting offended and changing his mind about Jesus.

When Jesus sent John's disciples back to tell John about the works He was doing, He ended his instruction with this small but life-changing statement, 'blessed is the one who is not offended by me' (Matthew 11:6). Jesus urged John to make a choice not to be offended in his heart but to keep believing the truth about who Jesus was, even though his circumstances made no sense. Jesus urged John to keep his focus on what was happening: 'the blind receive their sight and the lame walk, lepers are cleansed and the deaf hear, and the dead are raised up, and the poor have good news preached to them' (Matthew 11:5). When it came to things that had not yet happened, like his release from prison, Jesus encouraged John to lay down his right to understand and instead trust in God's understanding.

It is so easy for us to be like John, to focus on circumstances in our lives that make no sense and seem to contradict the truth about who God is. When we do, this offence can slowly take root in our hearts. It is so important we make a choice not to go there. If we can keep our hearts free from offence, we will ensure that God's Kingdom continues to flow through us. It is crucial that we discipline ourselves to keep focused on all the amazing things God is doing, rather than focusing on what is still to happen. This is a key principle in sustaining a naturally supernatural life.

BREAKTHROUGH IN THE MIDST OF MYSTERY

The Sunday after I came home from the hospital after my operation, I went to church and made a conscious decision to pray for the sick. There is something incredibly powerful about choosing to keep asking God for something when you are fighting your own battles and wrestling with unanswered questions in your own life. God has spoken to me about having an anointing to see breakthrough for women who suffer with problems in their wombs and ovaries, so I have made a deliberate decision to go after these conditions. As a result I have seen some significant miracles. A couple of years ago, I received an email from a lady we prayed for at a ladies' conference. She received prayer for some emotional pain and received some significant freedom. God healed her physically too. This is just part of her testimony:

I stood up after Wendy felt God say he wanted to help women with period problems or womb issues. I had terrible periods and cramps following the birth (of my daughter). I couldn't carry my daughter when the cramps started a week or so before my period. I would get a sharp stitch pain that was so intense I felt I had a knife in me. My periods when they actually started would be so heavy I couldn't leave the house for the day … My periods have now returned to normal! The cramp pain is non-existent and if I'm honest the pain is less than it was before having a baby! Hallelujah! Hardly any pain at all!

I am full of faith that these breakthroughs will continue to increase as I keep praying. In fact, if you are reading this and you need healing in your womb or ovaries right now: be healed in Jesus' name! I look forward to hearing how God breaks in.

In 2013, I had to have another operation. The cysts on my ovaries had grown back, and as a result of the surgery one of my ovaries was removed. I will share more about what happened later in the book, but suffice to say there was more disappointment to pray through.

Processing disappointment is a journey. Interestingly, the first miracle I saw after my second operation was a lump disappearing from a lady's breast.[5] I had been praying for cysts to disappear from my body, but still had to have surgery. This lady, who had been told she might need surgery, had a lump disappear when I prayed. I am so glad I did not allow offence to take root in my heart. I celebrated so much with this lady when she told me what God had done.

Even though there can often be a lot of mystery in our lives, God's nature does not change and it never will. The enemy will point at our circumstances to try and get us to believe lies about who God is, but our God never changes. Our God is perfect in every way, and He cannot be anything but perfect. Our God is always good and always working everything together for the good of those who love Him (Romans 8:28). In order to live the life God has called us to, the normal Christian life, we must pray for increased revelation of who He really is and what He is really like. We need revelation that impacts our hearts, not just our minds. And we must root out of our hearts any disappointment or offence that will attack this revelation.

Our God is eager to save the lost, heal the sick and set free the oppressed. It is His idea to use you and me to see His Kingdom break out on the earth. If you know you are living with disappointment, how about you carve out some time this week to intentionally work through it with God and allow the truth about who He is to go deeper in your heart?

NOTES

[1] Bethel Church is led by Bill Johnson. For more information, visit www.bethelredding.com.

[2] I do not profess to be putting an end to years of controversy surrounding this scripture. I am simply sharing the outcome of a personal encounter with God. Pursuing revelation of who God is and revelation of who He says I am has been a crucial part of my journey in living the life that Jesus modelled.

[3] Credit to Bill Johnson's teaching that has been the main influence in my journey of understanding how to process disappointment.

[4] I have talked about dealing with disappointment through my own experience of not being healed miraculously. You can use the same process for any area of disappointment in your heart: job situation, family, singleness, marriage, kids, finances. The list goes on.

[5] You can watch the story online at http://www.kingsarms.org/resources/media/message/breast-lump-disappears.html.

3
KNOW WHO
YOU ARE

A few years ago, I had the privilege of going on an overseas ministry trip with a small team from the church. As part of the trip, our hosts took us to watch an international cricket match. As we pulled up outside the cricket ground, the host nation's team was walking past on their way to the practice nets to warm up before the game. A lady on our team urged the guy driving our car to park quickly. She wanted the opportunity to chat to the players about Jesus: she was convinced this was our chance to impact an entire nation with the gospel!

To be honest, my thoughts were consumed with where we were going to eat before the match got underway. I was hungry! My friend's conviction that this was a key opportunity for a nation-changing encounter took me by surprise. The way she was thinking was totally different to the way I was thinking. A person who has it in their mind that God might want to use them to impact famous cricket players has got to have had revelation of their identity in Christ; revelation of their value and significance and their ability to see God's Kingdom come wherever they go. A person who has conviction that their encounter with famous cricket players has the potential to impact an entire nation is thinking like a beloved daughter of the King!

As soon as our car was parked, my friend rushed out to speak to one of the team. She explained that we were Christians visiting from the UK, and asked if there was anyone injured on the team who we could pray for (she figured this was the easiest and most natural way to get God into the conversation). The player looked pretty bemused to begin with, but then told my friend that their team captain would not be playing in the match because he had a calf injury. My friend asked if the captain was around to be prayed for, but he was still inside. She told the player we would pray anyway. After a very short and, on my part, half-hearted prayer (I was still hungry), we made our way to a local restaurant to eat.

About a week later, one of our team was back in the UK relaying the story to a group of leaders in the church. One of the leaders started to search on his phone for any online news reports about the cricket captain we had prayed for. To his surprise, and mine, he found an article saying that the captain had impressed his coach and the medical team after recovering quicker than expected from his calf injury. I felt so convicted by my lack of enthusiasm to pray in the moment. God really does want to use His people to impact nations!

THE BATTLE FOR IDENTITY

In the previous chapter, we looked at the importance of really knowing who God is if we want to live a naturally supernatural life. It is equally important to really know who He says we are. Matthew 16 reports that Peter received revelation from the Father about who Jesus was – 'You are the Christ, the Son of the living God' (v. 16). God spoke to me as I spent time reading this passage that it is this revelation that the church will be built on. Revelation of who Jesus is and therefore revelation of the Father; if you have seen Jesus, you have seen the Father (John 14:9). But the church will also be built on revelation of who Jesus says we are, our identity in Christ.

After Jesus congratulates Peter on the revelation he received, He tells Peter who he is: 'And Jesus answered him, "Blessed are you, Simon Bar-Jonah! For flesh and blood has not revealed this to you, but my Father who is in heaven. *And I tell you, you are Peter…*"' (vv. 17,18, italics mine). I remember asking God why this was included in the text. I was confused as to why Jesus made a specific point of telling Peter who he was at that moment. It was then that the Holy Spirit spoke to me about this revelation being an equally important part of the rock the church will be built on. The rock the church will be built on includes revelation of our brand new identity in Christ.

In order to see God's Kingdom come wherever we go, it is important to receive revelation of who Jesus says we are. The truth is that the second we give our lives to Jesus, we receive an identity transplant. The old sinful us dies and we became brand new creations, without blemish and free from accusation. Whatever you believe about yourself on the inside will affect how you behave on the outside. When Christians get revelation of who they really are in Christ, they become an unstoppable force. Christians who know their identity expect to be used by God to see His Kingdom come through them. It is because this revelation is so important in the mobilisation of the church that the enemy has chosen to wage war against it.

It was the enemy's tactic right at the beginning of Jesus' ministry to go after His identity. The Father affirmed Jesus and reminded Him who He was at His baptism. 'You are my beloved Son; with you I am well pleased' (Mark 1:11). The Holy Spirit then immediately led Jesus into the wilderness, where He was tempted by the devil. The first thing the enemy came to undermine and call into question was Jesus' identity. '*If you are the Son of God,* command these stones to become loaves of bread' (Matthew 4:3, italics mine).

The enemy loves to undermine and call into question our identity too. He and his workforce feed us lies about anything and everything; how we look, what people think about us, our abilities, our significance, how well we are following Jesus. The culture we live in and the broken people around us often reinforce these lies. The enemy also loves to point to and highlight hidden things in our lives that we are ashamed of and have never told anyone. The battle does not subside when we are having a hard time. The enemy does not feel compassion when Christians fall; he is prowling around looking for people to devour (1 Pt. 5:8). The sad truth is that so many in the church are listening to and choosing to believe the lies rather than believing the truth about who God says they are.

Knowing who God says I am and living in the good of it has been one of the areas of greatest battle for me. When I first became a Christian, I lacked confidence and I was very insecure. I did not like who God had made me to be and I thought that being a woman meant that I was weak and insignificant. The lies I believed made it difficult for me to enjoy my femininity and meant I spent most of my time hiding behind the mask of achievement. Pleasing other people was my top priority and it was not OK for me to make mistakes.

Over the years I have known incredible healing and freedom as I have received greater revelation of God's pleasure over me. I am learning to love who God has made me to be and I am realising how powerful and significant I am. If hearing me say this makes you squirm a bit on the inside, then this chapter is going to be key for you. I no longer hide behind what I do, or spend all my energy trying to make everyone around me happy. Instead, I am discovering what it means to be comfortable in my own skin. People often comment on how relaxed and secure I look when I speak publicly. This is testimony to the grace of God in my life. As I have grown in my understanding of God's love for me, my heart has been better positioned to receive revelation of the truth about my identity in Christ. This in turn has propelled me in my desire to see people encounter the love and power of God through the way I live my life.

I like to imagine what the church would look like if every believer really grasped that what God says about them is actually the truth. Many believers know the truth in their heads, but it is important that we go on a journey of receiving revelation of the truth that impacts our hearts. A key part of this journey is making a conscious decision to let the truth about our identity in Scripture drown out the lies of the enemy. I believe that Jesus' ability to stand firm in His Sonship in the wilderness was key to Him being able to fulfil His purpose on the earth. I believe the same is true for us. Our ability to stand firm in our identity is key to us being able to effectively fulfil our purpose on the earth and to see God's Kingdom come wherever we go.

CALLED TO BE SIGNIFICANT

There was something about hanging out with Jesus that made the disciples believe they were meant to have a significant impact on the earth: that they were called to be great. Luke 9 records James and John asking Jesus if they should call down fire from heaven to destroy a Samaritan village. The village had rejected Jesus and this was going to be the disciples' way of dealing with it. Of course they got it all wrong, Jesus came to save the lost, not destroy them. Yet their faith in their ability to actually call down fire from heaven in the first place is a provocation to me. They knew the extent of what was possible for them because they were with Jesus. On another occasion an argument started among the disciples about which of them was the greatest. Again the disciples were misguided, but Jesus did not tell them they should stop wanting to be great. Instead He showed them what true greatness looked like by pointing to the example of a child (Luke 9:46–48).

Children understand how amazing they are, but not in a proud or arrogant way. I have a beautiful goddaughter called Rae who has taught me so much about my identity. When she was three, she prayed this one evening, 'Dear God, I love you so much and I love myself. You are so good and I am so good.' On another occasion she wrote in my birthday card, 'I love myself.' I love this! As we get older we tend to lose this awareness of our value and significance and the result is that we step back and start to hide. The truth is we have incredible value and significance because God says so. The value of something is determined by the price someone is willing to pay to purchase it. God paid the ultimate price to purchase you and me by sending Jesus to the cross. The more we understand our identity as beloved children of God, the more we can step into our significance and influence from a place of humility and dependence on Him.

All of us have a unique role to play in seeing God's rule and reign established wherever we have influence. Seeing the sick healed, the dead raised, the spiritually oppressed set free and the lost saved is meant to be the normal Christian life for every believer. It is part of our spiritual DNA that came alive in us when we said yes to Jesus. Whether we are called to impact a homeless man on the streets, a group of mums at the school gate or an entire nation, knowing who God says we are is crucial. Receiving revelation of our identity in Christ and living in the good of it will mobilise us as we seek to make Jesus known wherever we go.

The truth about who we are in Christ is way too big for our minds alone to comprehend. Our new nature is described in Scripture as being holy and blameless, without blemish and free from accusation. We have been fashioned by God with incredible care and attention and our bodies are now temples of the Holy Spirit. We are described as being seated with Christ in heavenly places with access to heaven's resources. We are ambassadors of Christ, able to operate with His authority on the earth, and the same power that raised Jesus from the dead lives in us. We are loved and delighted in by the King of Kings and Lord of Lords. This is just some of what the Bible tells us. Simply trying really hard to believe these truths will not change our behaviour in the long term. We need revelation from God, a work of the Holy Spirit, for the truth about who we are to impact our hearts.

RECEIVING REVELATION

I have become aware over the years of a variety of ways we can intentionally prepare our hearts to receive revelation from God. The following lessons I have learnt are not a tick list to life change. Revelation is a work of the Spirit, and the most powerful thing we can do is pray and ask God for it. By intentionally pursuing the tips that follow, you can posture your heart to be increasingly open to the revelation God wants to bring.

1) Refuse to speak negatively about yourself

'Death and life are in the power of the tongue' (Proverbs 18:21). The words that come out of our mouths have power. Inherent in the words God speaks is the power to produce life. We see this at the beginning of Genesis when God created the world. 'And God said, "Let there be light", and there was light' (Genesis 1:3). God spoke and matter that did not exist previously came into existence. God's words contained the power to create what He declared. We are created in the image of God. The words we speak, like His, contain power. We can use our words to produce and create life, for example when our encouragement of someone leads to them embracing and flourishing in a particular gift. Or we can use our words to produce and create death, for example when we speak harshly and it results in people losing confidence and withdrawing from us and others. If we want to grow in revelation of our identity in Christ, we must consciously use our words to reinforce the truth about who God says we are.

I think one of the biggest barriers to Christians living in the fullness of their identity in Christ is directly related to words we speak over ourselves. Often the way we speak about ourselves is more in line with the enemy's lies rather than the truth God says. We can be negative, critical, harsh and unforgiving. The words we speak often agree with the enemy more than they agree with God, and because our words have power we struggle to grasp who we really are in Christ. We must be careful to speak positive, truth-filled and life-giving words over ourselves. We must make a conscious decision to intentionally speak out the truth about who God says we are and what we are called to do. I am not saying we should not confess our sin to trusted friends, this is actually a key way we increasingly step into our God-given identity. I am not saying we should avoid being honest about battles we are fighting or circumstances we are finding difficult. I am saying we need to be careful to say things in a way that produces life and steers clear of death.

It can be dangerous to speak negatively about yourself at King's Arms. We are developing a culture that refuses to allow people to say things that reinforce lies about their identity. I remember once at TSM, students were sharing stories of what God had been doing in and through them the previous week. I noticed one of the students who rarely shared come up to join the story line and I was excited to hear what God had done. As this particular student got to the microphone, she started her story by suggesting that compared to all the other stories shared, hers was not really very significant. Her comment was met with audible disagreement from the rest of the TSM family, as they reminded this beloved daughter it was not OK for her to say that kind of thing. Of course her story was significant, it was about God doing something in her life and therefore worthy of celebration. I encouraged the student to start her story again, and this time she began by telling us she had something exciting and significant to share. She was met with huge applause from the rest of the students as she caught a greater glimpse of the truth about her significance as God's daughter.

2) Avoid the comparison trap

Another way to position yourself for greater revelation of who you are in Christ and to love who God has made you to be, is to avoid the snare of comparison. So many Christians are immobilised in their relationship with God because they use so much energy wishing they were less like themselves and more like someone else. Many believers are hindered from stepping into a naturally supernatural life because they believe other people are much more qualified and likely to be used by God than them. Comparison stops us being all God has called us to be and doing all He has called us to do.

There are only two possible outcomes of comparison and both have a negative impact. When you compare yourself with someone you feel superior to, it is easy to fall into pride. The Bible tells us God opposes the proud (James 4:6). When you compare yourself with someone you feel inferior to, it is easy to believe the lie that you are insignificant and that you do not have a unique role to play in seeing God's Kingdom come on the earth. Both the pride and the lies will stop you living in the fullness of your identity. Comparison will get in the way of you being all God has called you to be.

A key antidote to comparison is thanksgiving. Choosing to thank God for the way He has made us and the things He has called us to, turns our attention away from the temptation to compare. It is important that we take time to listen to the truth God speaks over us and celebrate the unique passions and gifts He has given us. God loves who He has made you to be; you are not meant to be anyone else. All of us have a significant part to play in seeing God's Kingdom advance on the earth, but the way this happens will look different for each of us. The number of different ways you can see God's Kingdom come is as varied as the number of people involved in bringing the Kingdom. Watch out for being tripped up by comparison. God has a unique adventure designed just for you.

3) Learn to receive encouragement

Learning to receive encouragement is another way we can

prepare our hearts to take in revelation of who we are in Christ. This might seem over-simplistic but my experience has taught me that many Christians struggle to be encouraged. Many times my encouragement of Christians has met with uncomfortable squirming, reduced eye contact, and them telling me a variety of reasons why what I am saying is not true. If we struggle to receive encouragement from people, we will struggle to believe the truth about who God says we are.

Receiving encouragement from someone about a prophetic word I bring is nothing in comparison to receiving the truth that I am holy and dearly loved by God (Colossians 3:12). Believing the truth that I am an ambassador of Christ (2 Corinthians 5:20) is on a whole different level to believing I am fun to be around. By learning to receive encouragement on a small scale, we position our hearts to receive and believe the incredible truth about our identity in Christ. We also open our hearts to allow God to speak truth to us through other people.

At TSM our students are taught how to receive encouragement as a standard part of the course. The tips we give are meant to be fun and there is always a lot of laughter after the initial encouragement squirms, but the impact is huge. The difference in the students' ability to receive encouragement at the end of the year compared to the beginning is incredible. Our first tip is that the student being encouraged must maintain eye contact with their encourager at all times. This helps the truth to really get into a person and impact their heart. Our second tip, after the encouragement is given, is to get the person being encouraged to 'suck up' the encouragement. In other words, they need to take the truth on board, to intentionally receive it rather than letting it bounce off them. Our last tip requires the student being encouraged to thank their encourager and then ask them if there is anything else they would like to say. This is often the bit that evokes the most squirming.

Some people may get concerned that this focus on helping people receive encouragement will lead to pride. People will get good at receiving encouragement, but in the process will get puffed up in their heart. Here is what we teach our students to do: receive the encouragement and thank the person giving it, then the next time you spend time with Jesus, offer the encouragement to Him as part of your worship. We all know that anything we are good at and any success we experience is all down to the grace of God in our lives. Receiving encouragement from peers and then offering it to God as worship is such a sweet exchange. We get built up and then we get to grow in love and gratitude for the one who makes it all possible. How are you doing at receiving encouragement?

4) Pursue authenticity

We are passionate at King's Arms about establishing a culture of authenticity. Firstly, authenticity looks like people being true to who God has made them to be. We do not want people to hide their gifts or passions because they think they do not fit or they should be more like someone else. We live with the conviction that everyone has a unique role to play in seeing God's Kingdom impact the planet and we try to create an environment where people feel safe to be fully themselves.

Secondly, authenticity looks like being open and honest about sin issues and struggles in our lives so we can walk into freedom. Scripture describes the enemy as the accuser of the brethren (Revelation 12:10). He loves it when we have things from our past or present that we are ashamed of and have never told anyone about. These hidden sins can be used to lie to us about our identity and tell us we are disqualified from the purposes of God. Of course, the enemy will do whatever he can to immobilise us. He will even try to use sins we have confessed and received forgiveness for to keep us trapped and ineffective. Pursuing authenticity means to talk to trusted friends about our temptations and sin and the accusations that are thrown at us. Pursuing authenticity means to walk in the light.

'But if we walk in the light, as he is in the light, we have fellowship with one another, and the blood of Jesus his Son cleanses us from all sin' (1 John 1:7). This scripture shows us that when we choose to walk in the light, there are two significant outcomes. Firstly, we get to enjoy real fellowship with each other. People cannot really love you until they really know you. By taking off our Christian masks and inviting people to see who we really are, we can enjoy a deepening of genuine community. Secondly, we get to enjoy God's forgiveness and know a cleansing from all unrighteousness. In other words, we get to enjoy freedom from the sin and shame the enemy uses to accuse us and hold us back. As soon as we bring things into the light, the power of the shame we feel is broken and the accusations of the enemy are silenced. When we walk in the light we get to enjoy God's grace and receive greater revelation of the truth of who we are in Christ.

I have engaged in many awkward conversations with trusted friends as I have been honest about areas of sin I am struggling with. Authenticity is not always fun, but it is always worth it. I have also had the privilege of people confessing things to me that they have never told anyone before. The freedom that follows is one of my favourite things to witness. People get revelation of God's amazing grace, they realise where they have believed lies and they start to listen to the truth about who God says they are.

I remember once at the end of a meeting I had been speaking at, a lady approached me saying she needed to confess something to me. She looked scared and heavy with shame. I sat down with her and encouraged her for being so courageous. I tried to maintain eye contact with her so she could see the compassion I felt for her as she told me her story. Later I asked her to write her story down:

I became a Christian when I was eighteen. I felt loved by God and genuinely believed He forgave all my sins, except one. Before I got saved I lived a very messed up life. One day I slept with a married man to get money. I felt so dirty afterwards but at the same time I just brushed it aside.

When I became a Christian this thing kept bugging me. For some reason I felt like it was a sin too big to take to the Father. I was ashamed and thought because of these few stupid minutes I was not fully qualified as a Christian.

The first time I heard Wendy speak she talked about the power of confession and knowing we are forgiven. I had never told anyone what I had done but somehow I got the courage to just let it out to Wendy and then one of my friends.

I remember feeling SO free after that! I experienced God's joy for the first time. Knowing that God really does forgive ALL sins gave me the courage to fully come before Him and receive His love. Now the enemy can no longer hold my past against me because I know I am completely forgiven. I have been full of God's joy ever since.

It was such a privilege to see this brave lady get so much freedom; to see shame broken off her life and to be able to speak truth over her about her identity. Shortly after the conference, she contacted me to tell me about an exciting opportunity she had on the streets to see God's Kingdom come. When you understand your identity in Christ, you start to live with a different mind-set. You get increasingly convinced that God wants to use you to see His Kingdom advance.

Who do you have in your life who knows everything about you and is cheering you on? If you do not have anyone, ask God to show you someone over the next few weeks you could ask, and then make a conscious decision to be completely authentic with them. Pursuing authenticity is key in positioning our hearts for greater revelation of the truth about our identity in Christ.

5) Accept that believing the truth about who God says you are is not pride

We are instructed in Scripture to clothe ourselves with humility because 'God opposes the proud but gives grace to the humble' (1 Peter 5:5). Humility is a big deal to God and so it needs to be a big deal to us. However, I think many Christians are in danger of having an incorrect understanding of what humility actually means.

Humility is not about making ourselves small or thinking of ourselves as insignificant compared to everyone else. Humility means to live in the fullness of our brand new identity in Christ, realising that it is all made possible because of Jesus. When you understand your identity in Christ is nothing to do with you but all to do with His grace, you cannot help but fall more in love with Him. As I have asked God for greater revelation of who

He says I am, rather than there being pride in my heart, I have experienced a growing sense of awe and wonder and gratitude towards my heavenly Father. The identity Jesus won for us on the cross is totally overwhelming, and it stands to reason that when someone grows in revelation of the magnitude of the truth, they cannot help but worship God with increased fervour and passion.

Believing the truth about who God says we are is not pride. I think Jesus gets way more glory when we step in to all He won for us on the cross. I do not think it glorifies God when His sons and daughters put themselves down or believe lies about themselves. I do not think it glorifies Him when His children want to be small and insignificant. Jesus paid the ultimate price so we could do the works that He did, and even greater things (John 14:12). I believe what makes God happy is His children believing the truth, and living in the good of what He says about them. How are you doing at receiving and living in your God-given identity?

There is a battle on for our identity. The enemy knows how powerful the church will be if every believer lives in the fullness of their identity in Christ. He knows how quickly and powerfully the Kingdom will advance, and so he has waged war on this truth to immobilise the church. The enemy has won some battles, but Jesus is the one who is ultimately victorious on our behalf. If you are a believer, your identity has been completely transformed by Jesus. What God says about you and the way He feels about you is the truth. As you position yourself for revelation of the truth, it will change the way you think, which in turn will change the way you live. You will learn to be like my friend who prayed for the cricket captain: you will know that with God it is possible to impact entire nations with the gospel.

Move forward in your journey today by identifying a lie you believe about yourself. If a lie is not immediately obvious, ask a friend to speak some truth to you and pay attention to which truth makes you squirm the most. Once you have identified a lie, spend some time with God repenting for believing it and choosing to break agreement with it. After you have dealt with the lie, replace it with the truth. Speak the truth over yourself out loud and repeat it a few times until it gets into your system. Why not use this truth to get started: you are significant and you are called and anointed to see God's Kingdom come on the earth. There are supernatural encounters waiting for you everywhere you go.

4

UNDERSTAND
THE KINGDOM

Some TSM students and I got to know a lady who worked in a cafeteria, after a few weeks of intentionally visiting her. On one particular occasion when we went to see how she was, the lady was on her lunch break and invited us to sit at her table. We spent time asking how she had been since we last saw her, and generally catching up. She told us she had been suffering with a bad back and that she was still in some pain. When we offered to pray for her, she was happy to accept.

As we were praying, God began to speak to me about giving her the £10 note in my pocket. It was the faintest of nudges, much like a thought that could easily have been dismissed. For a few seconds I wrestled internally with what God was saying. It did not feel very generous to give such a small amount of money, and I was nervous about the lady feeling embarrassed or awkward. The prompt did not go away, and so after we prayed I offered her the money, explaining that I felt God ask me to give it to her. Our friend's emotional reaction was unexpected. Immediately she put her head in her hands and tears began to form in her eyes. She kept repeating over and over again that she could not believe what was happening; she was clearly grateful for the gift. As we asked why the money meant so much to her, she went on to explain her situation.

Money was very tight for her family, so tight that they did not have any milk or bread in the house. She had spent time with God that morning talking to Him about Psalm 37, where it says that those who have lived a righteous life will never have to beg for bread. She was asking God if she had failed to live a righteous life because of the position she was in, no bread in the house and no money to buy any. God's answer to her was loud and clear that afternoon as He gave her the money she so desperately needed. God's Kingdom came with comfort, peace and joy as this much-loved lady realised she had been living a righteous life and that God would take care of her every need. The Kingdom also came with healing as the pins and needles the lady was feeling in her feet before we prayed disappeared.

Living a naturally supernatural life is about releasing God's Kingdom wherever you go. In order to do that it is important to understand what the Kingdom of God is and what it looks like when it comes. Until I heard teaching about the Kingdom, I thought it mainly consisted of seeing people healed and getting words of knowledge. As I have grown in my understanding of the Kingdom, through teaching and seeing God bless people like the lady in the cafeteria, I have learnt how rich and multifaceted it is. God is passionate about multiple aspects of His Kingdom breaking in simultaneously to transform people's lives and circumstances.

WHAT IS THE KINGDOM?

The Kingdom of God can be simply defined as the rule and reign of God over all He has made. When God's Kingdom comes, we experience what is true of heaven right here on the earth. The Kingdom of God reflects all that is true of its King.

When John the Baptist first came preaching that the Kingdom of God was at hand, it caused a major stir.[1] People went to him from Jerusalem and Judea and the whole region of the Jordan to confess their sins and be baptised (Matthew 3:5,6). The people of Jesus' day were quick to respond when they heard God's Kingdom was close, because they knew this was good news for them. They were living with promises about a King who was coming to save them, whose Kingdom would overthrow the oppression and affliction they were living under. God had been silent for many years, but now everything was about to change.

When Jesus appeared on the scene He took the baton from John the Baptist and went about proclaiming and demonstrating the good news of the Kingdom. The Kingdom was central to Jesus' life and ministry: He told parables about it (Matthew 13); He taught His disciples to pray for it (Matthew 6:10); He rebuked the Pharisees and Sadducees for missing it (Luke 11:37–44); He taught people how to enter it (Matthew 18:3); everywhere He went Jesus healed the sick and set free the spiritually oppressed (Matthew 4:23–25), and then He passed the baton on to His disciples to proclaim and demonstrate the Kingdom wherever they went (Matthew 10:5–8). Throughout His ministry, Jesus' major focus was on seeing His Kingdom advance on the earth. He wants it to be our major focus too.

In order to understand what the Kingdom looks like when it comes, it is helpful to know what Jesus was expecting. Jesus confirmed He was the Messiah the people had been waiting for when He read from the scroll of Isaiah in a synagogue in Nazareth. What He read was an extract from Isaiah 61, a prophecy about the Messiah that detailed what He would be anointed by the Holy Spirit to do. In other words, it unpacks some of what God's Kingdom looks like when it comes:

'The Spirit of the Sovereign LORD is on me,
because the LORD has anointed me
to preach good news to the poor.
He has sent me to bind up the broken-hearted,
to proclaim freedom for the captives
and release from darkness for the prisoners,
to proclaim the year of the LORD's favour
and the day of vengeance of our God,
to comfort all who mourn,
and provide for those who grieve in Zion –
to bestow on them a crown of beauty
instead of ashes,
the oil of joy
instead of mourning,
and a garment of praise
instead of a spirit of despair. …
(Isaiah 61:1–3, NIV UK 2011)

The astonishing truth is that the same Holy Spirit who anointed Jesus to advance the Kingdom also anoints us. That means the things that are true of Jesus in Isaiah 61 are also true of every believer!

There are seven things we can expect when the Kingdom of God comes. As you read through each section, let faith be stirred in your heart. You carry these things to give away to everyone you meet:

1) God's presence: 'The Spirit of the Sovereign Lord is on me'

When God's Kingdom comes, His presence comes. Jesus was

anointed with the Holy Spirit and power, and the same Holy Spirit anoints and lives inside of us. Wherever we go we carry the presence of God with us, so whenever we have an opportunity to see God's Kingdom come, we can be confident that the Holy Spirit will be quick to reveal Himself, if we ask Him.

Some of the most fun I have had on the streets has been when I have asked people the question, 'If God was real, would you like to meet Him?' I have asked the question as the Holy Spirit has prompted me, and every time people have encountered God's presence as I have prayed. I prayed for three teenage girls in the town centre once. We were standing in a very busy walkway, it was noisy and there were people everywhere. As I prayed a very simple prayer, asking God to meet with His daughters, it was like everything suddenly became quiet. When I asked the wide-eyed girls what they were feeling, all of them commented on the stillness. It was like God's presence came and enveloped us just for a moment. God loves to reveal Himself to people who do not yet know Him.

2) Justice: 'because the LORD has anointed me to proclaim good news to the poor'

When God's Kingdom comes, people experience justice. The Kingdom of God is good news to the poor, because justice insists that the poor and marginalised are given dignity and treated with honour. Jesus loves to choose those who are weak and considered the lowest in society to be great in His Kingdom. We get to see His Kingdom advance by loving, restoring and speaking out on behalf of people society has given up on. In addition to this, we carry the mandate to pray for God's justice to trump and overrule any and every aspect of injustice we see in society or the lives of people we meet.

When the King's Arms Project first met Dave (not his real name) he was homeless and living under a bridge in the town.[2] After a few months of sleeping rough, he got a bed at the Nightshelter, and soon after that he moved to more secure housing at Barton House hostel.

Through the Project, Dave started to connect with people who were keen to introduce him to Jesus. He met people who loved him and valued him and gave him time and a sense of purpose. Dave started attending King's Arms Church, and quickly found himself on a serving team. People in the church became like family to him, and it was not long before he made the decision to give his life to Jesus and get baptised. Dave now lives much more independently in one of our move-on houses. His life is totally different now:

I feel happy, alive! I'm working and meeting people. I wouldn't have been here if I didn't have the help from the people around me and God looking out for me. I'm full of energy and God has given me a new lease of life.

The Project has many stories like this one, where people forgotten and shunned by society have been loved and prayed back into a place of hope and destiny. The man who currently manages our Nightshelter used to sleep there as a resident! He was homeless, addicted to drugs and without hope, but our God rescued him and set him free. Now he lives to see others in the position he was in experience the unconditional love of their heavenly Father. This is the justice of the Kingdom.

3) Healing: 'He has sent me to bind up the broken-hearted'
When God's Kingdom breaks in, people get healed. Isaiah 61

tells us we are anointed by God to bind up the broken-hearted. When Jesus read the scripture over Himself in the synagogue, the mandate included physical healing as well, 'He has sent me to proclaim ... recovery of sight for the blind' (Luke 4:18). As ambassadors of Christ, we are called and anointed to see people healed emotionally and physically as we live the normal Christian life.

A friend of mine had the privilege of spending time with a lady she met in a coffee shop who clearly needed emotional healing. The lady struggled to carry her coffee to a table, and when my friend noticed she smiled sympathetically at the lady and asked if she was OK. The lady immediately opened up about her situation. She was a full-time carer for her mother who was suffering with dementia, and she had just come from bereavement counselling because her mother-in-law had died recently. My friend invited this hurting lady to sit at her table and what followed was a two-hour God encounter.

My friend sat and listened to the lady as she opened up about her life and what was going on in her heart. She talked about shame and guilt she was carrying, about a difficult relationship with her dad, her struggle to come to terms with loss in different areas of her life, and about several painful health issues she had. After quite a while, the lady began to ask my friend questions about her life. She was keen to know how my friend coped with difficulties. My friend was able to share some of her testimony, talk about her relationship with Jesus, and explain the gospel. When she offered to pray, the lady agreed, asking for prayer for something to change in her relationship with her dad. As my friend prayed, this broken lady began to cry as the Holy Spirit began to unravel the pain in her heart. After two hours, my friend left the lady with her number and details about the church.

My friend did not hear from the lady and we have not yet seen her at church, so we do not know what God has done since. What we do know is God came and met with a fragile lady in a coffee shop who was emotionally broken, and as His Kingdom came, a bit of her heart got healed up. Wherever we see broken hearts or broken bodies, we are anointed to see healing break in.

4) Salvation and Deliverance: 'to proclaim freedom for the captives and release from darkness for the prisoners'

When God's Kingdom comes, people get set free from spiritual oppression and come into the relationship with God they have been created for. The greatest miracle of all is when people are rescued out of darkness into light. Although I have only led two people all the way through to giving their life to Jesus on the streets (so far!), I have friends who have seen many responses to the gospel. Most encounters we have lead people closer to Jesus in some way. We may not always see people pray a prayer of salvation, but our moment with them may be utterly integral to them giving their life to Jesus a few months or years down the line. I am learning that seeing people come to know Jesus is easier than I thought. The truth is that the harvest is plentiful and our God is mighty to save.

When it comes to God's Kingdom breaking in with deliverance, we have seen many breakthroughs in the church, but our experience of seeing deliverance on the streets is a bit more sparse. Jesus saw lots of people set free as He went about His everyday life; He healed all who were under the power of the devil. I anticipate it is only a matter of time before this sign of the Kingdom becomes more commonplace outside of the church. God is passionate about His children receiving freedom from the grip of the enemy and knowing wholeness on the inside.

A friend of mine saw God's Kingdom come with deliverance when she noticed a lady collapse outside a house not too far from her. She rushed to the lady to make sure she was OK, and ended up praying for her for healing. This lady had suffered with ME since her father died three years earlier, and she had lost all feeling in one of her legs. She lived with constant pain. While my friend was praying, the lady started to cry and then she began to cough and retch as God's presence came on her. My friend knew that coughing and retching can sometimes be a sign that God is setting a person free from spiritual oppression, so she just kept praying for more of God's love to come. My friend encouraged the lady not to be afraid as she explained what was happening: 'Sometimes when God's love comes and fills us there is no longer any room for any bad stuff, so it has to come out.' By the time my friend said goodbye to this lady, she had been able to walk without pain, she had received incredible peace in her heart and she had given her life to Jesus! God's Kingdom comes with deliverance and salvation.

5) Peace: 'to proclaim the year of the LORD's favour'

It would be easy to put peace at the bottom of the pile when it comes to what you want God to release through you. It can seem unglamorous and lacking in any real power; the healing and salvation miracles sound much more fun! The truth is, people who do not know Jesus are desperate for peace. So many people are living with stress and anxiety in their hearts and minds, and it is having a negative impact on their health and overall quality of life. God's peace has the power to transform people on the inside, and impact any chaotic situations they may be facing. As Christians, we enjoy peace with God and carry His favour, which means we get to release peace wherever we go. When God's Kingdom comes, we can expect supernatural peace.

I remember being at the hospital talking to a mum outside the children's ward. She had two very cute children, one of whom was obviously ill. He was sitting in a pushchair looking quite pale, with a feeding tube up his nose. As we were talking, the toddler in the pushchair started to get a bit irritable. He started to fidget and cry out, and he seemed to be getting increasingly distressed. I knew I had God's peace in me to give away, so I crouched down next to the buggy and, while still speaking to the mum, put my hand on his leg to release peace. Within about thirty seconds, this adorable little boy had fallen asleep. I learnt something that day about the power of God's peace. Whenever we see the absence of peace in people's lives or situations we find ourselves in, we get to represent the Prince of Peace by bringing peace.

6) Comfort: 'to comfort all who mourn'

When God's Kingdom comes, people are comforted. As we have gone out on the streets over the years, we have met people who have had to walk through exceptionally tragic circumstances. Many people have experienced so much loss and pain in their lives that their hearts are wracked with grief. The wonderful truth is that God's comfort is more powerful than any grief someone might be carrying. You can meet someone who has encountered the most devastating loss and have faith that God's Kingdom comes with comfort that can result in healing and restored hope. I think one of my friends can explain the power of God's comfort better than me:

> In 2013, my husband and twelve-year-old son died in a walking accident in the Alps, leaving me and my fifteen-year-old daughter. At the time, I did not have the words or understanding to describe God's comfort. All I knew was that although I was in great pain, I had a peace, an amazing sense of hope and at times even joy. It was, given the circumstances, supernatural.
>
> Much of the comfort I received came from the people God placed around me and from His presence in my life. When I worshipped I sensed God's presence and knew that the God of the entire universe was with me.
>
> My biggest comfort was, and still is, from God's word. In Romans 15:4 the word translated 'encouragement' is actually a Greek word for comfort; the comfort we get from the Scriptures gives us hope. As I choose to trust in God's word hope comes, which in turn brings comfort to me even in the midst of my pain.

God's comfort is supernatural and it is powerful. When we meet people on the streets who have experienced tragedy and loss, we do not need to feel overwhelmed. Instead, we can be confident that when we pray, God's Kingdom will come to bring healing and restore hope.

7) Joy: 'to bestow on them … the oil of joy instead of mourning, and a garment of praise instead of a spirit of despair'

When God's Kingdom breaks in, people experience joy. The

Bible teaches that in God's presence there is 'fullness of joy' (Psalm 16:11), and that the joy of the Lord is our strength (Nehemiah 8:10). The joy God offers is not a temporary thing, like a laugh that lasts for a moment, although it can involve lots of laughter. God's joy is powerful, and it changes lives. When people experience supernatural joy, it is like something comes alive on the inside. God's joy brings lightness and wages war against worry, because it helps people see things from His perspective. The joy of the Kingdom stifles depression and gives people hope for the future.

A lady in our church was diagnosed with depression when she was fifteen and started taking antidepressants when she was thirty. During her down times it was a challenge for her to interact with people, and sleep was a continual struggle. Not long after she gave her life to Jesus, she received prayer for healing at one of our conferences. She used to take her antidepressants at the same time as some other medication so she would not forget it, but about six weeks after the conference she realised she had forgotten to take the tablets. She knew God had done something because usually she would experience side effects if she missed any medication, and she was feeling good emotionally. God healed a forty-year battle with depression, and the result has been immense amounts of joy. As the Kingdom has come with joy, this beautiful lady's life has been completely turned around.[3]

The Kingdom of God is so rich and multifaceted. Whenever we see the opposite of these aspects of the Kingdom we have just looked at, we are commissioned and anointed by God to pray for breakthrough. The challenge for many Christians and churches is to do with our focus. Jesus said He will build His church and that our job is to extend His Kingdom. Sadly, we can often be so focused on how the church is doing that advancing the Kingdom gets put on the back burner. I love the promise in Habakkuk about the earth being 'filled with the knowledge of the glory of the LORD as the waters cover the sea' (Habakkuk 2:14). I believe God's Kingdom advancing is one of the main ways His glory will cover the earth. Understanding what the Kingdom of God looks like is a crucial step on the journey of living a naturally supernatural life. Equally important is being aware of how the Kingdom works: the 'now and not yet' of the Kingdom.

KINGDOM 'NOW' AND 'NOT YET'

The Kingdom of God is both 'now' and 'not yet'. When Jesus started His ministry, the Kingdom of God burst onto the scene. When He died on the cross and rose again victorious, He defeated the enemy and accomplished everything necessary for God's Kingdom to come in all its fullness. When Jesus comes back, there will be a new heaven and a new earth and God will dwell among His people. 'He will wipe away every tear from their eyes, and death shall be no more, neither shall there be mourning, nor crying, nor pain any more, for the former things have passed away' (Revelation 21:4). Jesus is going to make all things new, but as we wait for that day we live in this in-between time. God's Kingdom has come, is here and is continually advancing, but is not yet here in all its fullness.

When some people teach about the Kingdom they over-emphasise the 'not yet'. Understanding there is a 'not yet' aspect to the Kingdom is really important. It helps us realise we will not always see the breakthroughs we are asking God for this side of heaven, which enables us to navigate disappointment well. When the enemy tries to lie to us about the nature of God, understanding the 'not yet' of the Kingdom means we can face mystery, but still hold firmly to the truth that God is perfectly good and cannot be anything but good. For example, the fact that my cysts did not disappear supernaturally does not mean that God was not able or willing to heal, nor that He does not love me. It is part of the mystery of the 'not yet' of the Kingdom. Understanding the 'not yet' of the Kingdom is really helpful, but overemphasising it above the 'now' of the Kingdom is wrong. I believe many who overemphasise the 'not yet' of the Kingdom do so because they are living with disappointment and unbelief.

Jesus lived with a major emphasis on the Kingdom being 'now'. Everywhere He went, He talked about and demonstrated the Kingdom, and He taught us to persevere in prayer for breakthrough and not give up (Luke 18:1–8). When I teach about the Kingdom I like to teach about the 'not yet', but emphasise and build faith for the 'now'. Some people may be fearful of an overemphasis on the 'now'; they might feel it sets people up for unnecessary pain and disappointment. For some it is a particular challenge when praying for unbelievers who have no frame of reference for working through disappointment with God. They might be concerned that an encounter that does not lead to breakthrough will make it difficult for people to believe in a good God, and maybe turn them away from Him. My experience has taught me that if your primary motivation is to love the person in front of you, whether they experience supernatural breakthrough or not, they are always grateful for your time and prayers.

When I get to heaven, I do not think Jesus is going to say I expected too much of Him. To be honest, I am often convicted that the opposite will be true, and that there is much more breakthrough to be had. I would rather live my life expecting too much and have to work through some disappointment than expect too little and not see God's Kingdom advance as I could. I have a way to go with my expectation levels, but I am on a journey of growing in faith, holding onto the truth that 'with God all things are possible' (Matthew 19:26).

IMPACTING SOCIETY

At King's Arms, our experience of God's Kingdom breaking in started in the church during our Sunday meetings. We decided to be intentional about bringing words of knowledge and praying for the sick every week, and it was not long before we regularly saw people healed and set free. After a while of seeing God's Kingdom come in the church, we realised we also needed to be intentional about seeing breakthrough 'on the streets'. The Kingdom of God is not meant to stay within the four walls of the church. Like yeast working its way through an entire batch of dough, the Kingdom is meant to reach and influence every area of society (Matthew 13:33). 'Of the greatness of his government and peace there will be no end' (Isaiah 9:7, NIV UK 2011). We are seeing God's Kingdom impact society in Bedford and beyond as we are growing in courage and learning how to live the normal Christian life.

Healthcare

We have people in our church impacting the healthcare sector as they are obedient to promptings from God. One particular lady works on a ward with patients who suffer with severe mental illness. During an annual appraisal with her boss, she was asked what she wanted to achieve in the next year.

She talked about how treatment on the ward focused on the mind and body of patients, but that there was no focus on their spiritual wellbeing. She told her boss she would like to be the person in charge of spiritual input for the patients, even though she was sure it would not be allowed. About a week later, this brave lady received an email agreeing to her request; a new role was created to make her spiritual leader for the ward! This amazing lady is an incredible prayer warrior, and often prays for staff and patients. She is passionate about seeing people set free from mental illness, and although she has not yet seen any immediate breakthrough, we know her prayers are powerful and effective.

Education

We have people involved in education who are taking opportunities to make Jesus known in their workplace. Often these opportunities are one-on-one conversations with pupils and staff, but one particular story stands out, when a teacher got to see God's Kingdom come with a whole class. She was teaching a philosophy lesson, where she got to talk about Jesus and the fact that He heals today. She asked if any of the students needed healing, and one of them said he had pain in his thumb. The teacher prayed once but seemingly nothing happened,[4] so she encouraged the rest of the class to gather round the boy and pray with her. To everyone's surprise, the pain in the boy's thumb immediately disappeared. Suddenly all the students who were sick wanted prayer. The teacher paired the students off, quickly did some coaching on how to pray for the sick, and then let them have a go. Many of the students said the pain they had been feeling got better. The teacher saw an open door to give the gospel and ask if any of the students wanted to give their lives to Jesus. Around seventeen of the students put their hands up to respond.[5]

Business

We also have people who are seeing God's Kingdom impact businesses. One lady runs her own leadership coaching company. She is fulfilling her dream to go into businesses and teach Jesus leadership and Kingdom culture, mainly using secular language. She has many stories of how God has used her to impact individuals and teams. Most of her opportunities to see God's Kingdom come are 'covert'. She will ask people questions based on what God is showing her prophetically, but not talk about the fact that what she is hearing is from God. Sometimes, though, when led by the Holy Spirit, she openly talks about her faith. On one particular occasion, God told her He had created the man she was coaching to be an inventor. When she told the man 'the thought in her head', he was shocked; he loved to invent things and asked my friend how she knew. She felt prompted to tell him outright that God had told her. The conversation opened up further dialogue about the goodness of God.

We are seeing Jesus revealed in many other areas of society as people in our church family take hold of the mandate to see God's Kingdom come wherever they go: a group in the church are serving Bedford prison and seeing prisoners give their lives to Jesus through Alpha; another group are focusing on impacting the music scene in Bedford pubs; there are people in the church championing adoption and fostering, and wanting to see families thrive with God at the centre; there are people passionate about serving the poor, and others who want to connect with those leading in local and national government. Slowly but surely, God's Kingdom is advancing and many individuals and areas of society are hearing about and encountering the kindness of God.

Jesus modelled the normal Christian life, proclaiming and demonstrating the Kingdom wherever He went. He has now passed the baton on to us. We are anointed with the same Holy Spirit who anointed Jesus, which means seeing the Kingdom come is in our DNA. We do not have to strive or strain to see breakthrough. The key is learning to follow Jesus really closely, so that what He has already put inside us can naturally flow out. There will be mystery to work through along the way, when God seems silent and our prayers seem ineffective. What is important in these moments is that we persevere in prayer without lowering our expectation. The truth is that God is passionate about His Kingdom coming, He is not indifferent about it or reluctant in any way, and one day we will get to enjoy God's Kingdom in all its fullness. As we wait for that glorious day, let us make the most of every opportunity to represent Jesus wherever we go, to reveal the King by releasing His Kingdom.

'The Spirit of the Sovereign LORD is on me'; therefore let us go on a journey of really believing this truth, allowing it to grow our confidence as we aspire to live a naturally supernatural life. Which area of society do you feel called to influence with the Kingdom? Ask God for your eyes to be opened this week to an opportunity to see His Kingdom break in.

NOTES
[1] In the Gospel of Matthew, John is recorded as saying the Kingdom of

Heaven is at hand. The Kingdom of God and the Kingdom of Heaven are the same thing.

[2] King's Arms Project is a ministry of King's Arms Church. It is a Christian registered charity set up to work with the homeless in Bedford. For more information, see their website: www.kingsarmsproject.org.

[3] Watch the full story on our website http://www.kingsarms.org/resources/stories-and-testimonies/message/healing-of-allergies-and-depression.html.

[4] We encourage people to say 'seemingly nothing happened' rather than 'nothing happened', because sometimes you cannot see what God has done. Our words are powerful, and we do not want to undermine something God may have done by saying He did nothing.

[5] There are a lot of restrictions in place for teachers, and many other professionals, when it comes to talking about Jesus and offering to pray for people in their workplace. When I was a teacher I learnt the importance of recognising and responding to promptings from the Holy Spirit, and then trusting God with the outcome of my obedience.

5
BE MOTIVATED
BY LOVE

I remember several years ago speaking at a church and sharing some very specific words of knowledge that turned out to be right. One of the words was about a knee injury, and I prayed for a man who responded. I cannot remember if the man was healed or not because I was not really thinking about him at the time. I was just excited I had heard God so clearly. Of course, it is good to celebrate when you hear God clearly, but not at the expense of loving the people who respond to the words. When I spent time with God later in the week, He convicted me of how little I had focused on the guy with the bad knee. I had been more excited about getting an accurate word of knowledge than loving the person who responded to it. I spent time repenting and asking God to change my heart, and I have been on a journey of growing in love for people ever since. I am learning that love is the best motivation for seeing sustained supernatural breakthrough.

It is possible to have so many other motivations for living a naturally supernatural life other than love. We can pray for the sick because it is what we ought to do as Christians rather than because we feel compassion for a person. We can speak to people about Jesus because we are meant to 'do evangelism' rather than because we feel God's love for someone. We can ask God for accurate words of knowledge because we want a good story to tell to validate our walk with God or impress other people. In addition to this, many Christians carry guilt and shame because they feel they are not doing enough to lead people to Jesus. When you pursue the normal Christian life out of a place of guilt, people are likely to become projects. If these people fail to respond to God the way you want them to, you are likely to quickly lose motivation. Being motivated by guilt in evangelism could also make you more susceptible to burnout, distance from God and a hard heart. But when you pursue the normal Christian life because you are motivated by love, it changes everything.

God has created every human being with great care and attention (see Psalm 139). People we meet who do not yet know Jesus have been made in God's image. He loves them and they have incredible value and worth, and our job is to show them just how loved they are. When you understand that your main role in living a naturally supernatural life is to demonstrate God's love and kindness to everyone you meet, it takes the pressure off you having to make something happen. Love can look like so many different things: buying someone a coffee; prophesying over someone; offering to carry someone's shopping; sitting with someone for a few hours so they can chat. The ultimate aim when people meet you is that they get a glimpse of what God is like: that He is love (1 John 4:8); that He is kind; that He is a perfect Father. When love is your motivation, speaking to people about Jesus becomes a joy and a privilege and is much more likely to become part of your everyday life.

One of our TSM outreach teams met a guy on the streets who

was homeless. He was a contact of the King's Arms Project, had been out of town for ten years, and had come back to Bedford the night before our team met him. Over the course of about two hours, our students had the privilege of showing him his value and worth. They spent time listening to him as he told them about his life, about friends and family he had lost, and about the poetry he wrote. They laughed with him, connected with his sorrow, and pointed out things he was good at. They bought him a coffee and some food, some gloves, a scarf and some new shoes, and they shielded him from embarrassment in the shoe shop when people saw how dirty his socks were. One of the TSM team phoned the Nightshelter to see if a bed was available, because this guy had slept on the streets the night before. A group of beloved sons and daughters, saved by grace, got to communicate and demonstrate God's love to another beloved son. This is what love looks like. The guy ended up getting a bed at the Nightshelter, and found his way to church the following morning.

MOVED WITH COMPASSION

Jesus was motivated by love. Out of the overflow of His powerful love for humankind flowed a deep compassion that moved Jesus to release His Kingdom wherever He went. It was compassion that moved Jesus to heal the sick and set free the oppressed (Matthew 14:14). His love and compassion for people stirred Jesus to feed the hungry and reinstate the outcast and raise the dead (Luke 7:13–15). Jesus' love for people resulted in compassion that moved Him to action, and the breakthrough that resulted is still impacting the world today.

Compassion is a powerful emotion. The Greek root word refers to feelings that produce movement or action. Compassion elicits a response from the person feeling it. When I first started speaking to people on the streets, I prayed regularly that God would increase my courage. I still pray for courage, but I have learnt over the years to also ask God for increased compassion. When you connect with how God feels about the people you come into contact with, it is difficult to be indifferent and ignore what you see. Compassion stifles fear and gets you to a place where you cannot help but respond to what you feel.

Some people's response to a tough situation is filled with despair and hopelessness. These feelings can still move them to try to bring comfort or support, but they will be trying to make a difference with little or no expectation of anything changing. As Christians, we get to respond with faith to the compassion we feel. We can be moved into action and believe that what we do can make a difference, and that even seemingly hopeless situations can change. The truth is that with Jesus there is always hope, because He is in charge and always has the last word. When we see a need for God's Kingdom to break in and we are moved by compassion mixed with faith, anything is possible.

A TSM student had to go to the doctors' surgery one Christmas Eve to get some medication. While she was there, a lady walked in who was clearly suffering with severe back pain. The student immediately felt compassion for her and knew she needed to offer to pray for her before she left. As the student went to get her prescription, she passed the lady and explained she was a Christian. She asked the lady if she could pray for her and ask Jesus to take away her pain. The lady agreed; she was desperate. As our student prayed, compelled by compassion, this lady who was experiencing intense pain powerfully encountered the presence of God. 'That was spooky!' were the first words out of her mouth. When asked how her back was, the lady grabbed our student's arm and, with tears rolling down her face, told her it was better. She was exceptionally grateful for the relief from pain. The Kingdom of God came in a doctors' surgery on Christmas Eve because one of our students connected with God's heart for a lady who was suffering.

PERSONAL COMFORT VERSUS BRINGING THE KINGDOM

The challenge many of us face on the journey of being motivated by love and moved with compassion is to allow our hearts to connect with the love God feels for the people we meet. Compassion is a powerful motivator, but it is not always comfortable. One of the culture traits I notice in Western Christians is that many of us seem to prioritise the pursuit of personal comfort above our pursuit of the Kingdom. Jesus teaches us to 'Seek the Kingdom of God above all else, and live righteously, and he [the Father] will give you everything you need' (Matthew 6:33, NLT).

Many of us live in a culture that prioritises personal comfort, where the ability to comfort ourselves is at our fingertips. Some people seek comfort in owning a nice house, or buying fashionable clothes, or watching movies, or surfing the net. Other people might turn to drugs, or alcohol, or unhealthy relationships. Comfort looks different for different people, but the underlying motivation in all of us is the desire to live more comfortable lives. Many of us think that feeling uncomfortable is to be avoided at all costs, so we do everything we can to pursue quick-fix comfort. In doing so, many of us are unwittingly comforting ourselves to death.

Over time, our hearts get increasingly disconnected from God and we gradually lose the ability to feel. Any outreach we do lacks genuine feeling for the people we meet and can quickly become a tick box exercise.

The truth is that God never promised we would be comfortable. What He did promise was a Comforter, the Holy Spirit (John 14:16). God's plan is that we go to Him for the comfort we need, rather than looking for it in other places. When we go to God for comfort, our hearts can stay soft and connected and able to feel His love and compassion for the people we meet. Going to God also means we are more likely to stay in a place of faith for the Kingdom to break in and for our action to bring change. Feeling God's love and compassion for others is not always comfortable, but it is so much better than feeling numb on the inside.

Some of our TSM students used to go fairly regularly to pray around the grounds of the hospital. We have such a lot of respect for the hospital staff and chaplaincy team, who do a brilliant job caring for people. We just felt stirred to go and see if God wanted to open up any opportunities for us to share His love with the people we met. Over the course of a few years, we saw God do some incredible things. On one occasion, we got chatting to a lady sitting on a bench outside A&E who had ruptured her Achilles tendon. The damage was going to take about six weeks to heal, and she was in quite a bit of pain, with restricted movement. She was really open to prayer, and was visibly surprised by what God did. By the time we had finished praying, the pins and needles she had in her toes had gone, the pain she felt shoot up her leg whenever she put her foot down stopped, and she was beginning to get increased movement in her ankle. As we talked to this dear lady, she opened up to us about how she had stopped attending church after her nan died suddenly a few years earlier. We had the privilege of telling her how much God loved her, before her dad came to pick her up.

Even though we saw God open up many opportunities for us to bless people, being around the hospital was not comfortable. Everywhere we went, there were people who suffered terribly on a daily basis. We went with faith because we knew Jesus was the answer for every patient, every visiting friend and family member, and every member of staff. We went with hope, joy and expectation of breakthrough, knowing that God wants His Kingdom to impact every person on the planet. We also tried to keep engaging with the discomfort of compassion. It would have been easy to withdraw our hearts and become desensitised to the suffering we saw, but I would honestly choose experiencing compassion and feeling uncomfortable over feeling numb every time. I have found that the more I connect with feelings in my heart, the more alive I feel in my relationship with God.

Over the years, God has taken me on a journey of increasingly connecting my heart with His. I am learning what it means to love people like Jesus loves them. I am still very much on a journey, and I still go through seasons when I struggle to feel God's love and compassion for the lost. During one particular season like this, God spoke to me through the autobiography of Charles Finney. Finney was an American minister and revivalist in the 1820–30s. The book tells a story of when Finney was asked to say grace before a meal. There were two unbelievers at the table and Finney became so overwhelmed with compassion for them that he was unable to finish his prayer.

I had scarcely more than begun before the state of these young people rose before my mind and excited so much compassion that I burst into weeping and was unable to proceed. Everyone around the table sat speechless for a short time while I continued to weep.[1]

After a while of sitting awkwardly at the table, one of the men who was not a Christian left the table and fled to his room. When he came out of his room the next morning he had given his life to Jesus!

Finney was asked to say grace before a meal, but became so overwhelmed with compassion for the non-Christians at the table that he ended up weeping. As I read this story, and others throughout the book, I felt inspired and challenged. I could not remember the last time I had wept for my unbelieving friends and family, let alone two strangers I happened to be having dinner with. Through Finney's story, God provoked me to ask some questions about why my heart lacked love and compassion for the lost. As God has taken me on a journey of reconnecting my heart, the love and compassion I feel for people now is on a completely different level to where it used to be.

GETTING CONNECTED

Love and compassion are the best motivators for following in the footsteps of Jesus, but you do not have to wait until you feel God's perfect love for someone to step out and have a go at bringing His Kingdom. If you did, you might be waiting a long time. The key is to be obedient to the promptings of the Holy Spirit; often our hearts connect as we choose to say yes to Him. You cannot muster up love and compassion overnight, nor should you feel pressure to. Growing in love and compassion is a work of the Holy Spirit, and a journey. Irrespective of how connected you feel right now, whether it is easy for you to feel love and compassion or a challenge, here are a few thoughts on how to take some steps forward on your journey.

1) Receive God's love and compassion for you

'We love because he first loved us' (1 John 4:19). In other words, any love we have for those around us flows out of revelation and experience of the love God has for us. The more I know how much God loves me, the more I am able to love others. Bob Johnson in his book, *Love Stains*, puts it this way: 'Loving people the way Jesus loved comes from knowing just how loved you are yourself.'[2]

At King's Arms, we run a Father Heart Conference every year. During the conference, we learn about who God is as our Father and who we are as His sons and daughters. We have opportunities to work through pain we are carrying that stops us being able to receive God's love, and often lies we believe are exposed and broken. Over the course of the conference we get to spend lots of time in God's presence, encountering His love for us. You cannot help but go away changed.

These conferences have had a major impact on our ability to love well. They have impacted our love for God, our love for ourselves and each other, but also our love for those we meet on the streets. The way many of us love people now is different because of how we have experienced God's love for us at these conferences. With each new revelation of God's love for us we are increasingly able to be motivated by love as we seek to represent Jesus to the world around us.[3]

Being moved by compassion works in the same way. The

more you understand the compassion God has for you, the more you are likely to feel compassion for those around you. God is full of compassion for us (Psalm 145:8). He wants to show us compassion in the areas of sin we struggle with and the relational problems we are facing. He wants us to receive His compassion for the sickness we are battling with and the grief we are walking through. God has infinite compassion for us, but we do not always take time to allow ourselves to receive it.

I remember being in a worship time at TSM where God clearly spoke to us about receiving His compassion. We had been worshipping for about an hour, and God's presence was with us in such a gentle and intimate way. God began to speak to me about the importance of us knowing His compassion for us if we wanted to feel compassion for others. I shared what He said from the front and encouraged the students and team to open their hearts to God to receive from Him. There were tears all around the room as people, many for the first time, actually became aware of God's compassion for them. It was one of those moments where nobody needed to pray or prophesy. God came and hearts were softened and changed.

Receiving God's love and compassion for you is one of the main ways you will grow in love and compassion for those around you. Why not take some time with God today where your only agenda is to let Him love you and show you His compassion? When you have done it once, aim to make it a regular discipline in your life and see how it influences the love and compassion you feel for others.

2) Allow God to use your own battles and suffering

God has used my own battle with sickness to grow the love

and compassion I feel for others. After my first operation in 2007, my consultant informed me that cysts grow back in 50 per cent of cases. I remember thinking to myself that I was not going to be on the wrong side of that statistic. During the summer of 2013, I had some pain in my abdomen, so I decided to get it checked out. It was a routine check-up so I did not expect the consultant to find anything, but after a series of tests he told me that the cysts had grown back on both ovaries and there was risk again it could be cancer. I was totally devastated. The consultant's recommendation was that I have both ovaries removed.

The month between hearing the news and the operation was extremely tough. I had to decide what to ask the consultant to do during the operation. Should I go along with his recommendation to remove both ovaries, which would mean I could never have children, or ask him to save them, running the risk of further surgery if the cysts were cancerous? So many people were praying, and although I was regularly battling with a lot of fear and confusion, I managed to get to a place of faith that God would do a miracle. I decided to ask the consultant to save the ovaries if he could, and we began to pray that both cysts would disappear supernaturally and that there would be no trace of cancer.

I had the operation on 23 October 2013. The cysts had not supernaturally disappeared and the consultant had to remove one of my ovaries. My recovery time was a very dark season. I was gutted about the outcome of the surgery and had to endure several weeks of feeling very sick. On top of the physical pain was the emotional and spiritual turmoil. I struggled to connect with God for weeks after my surgery, and I was wracked with a deep sense of grief for the loss of my ovary. When I got a letter though the post two weeks into my recovery telling me that tests on the cysts showed no traces of cancer, I sat on my sofa and wept with relief. Looking back, I feel convinced that God did something amazing as a result of all the prayers prayed. Although the cysts did not disappear as I had hoped, I am sure that the outcome of the surgery was much better than it could have been. I know God intervened and maybe one day I will get to see the extent of His intervention.

Although I do not think it is necessary for us to go through hard circumstances to be able to love people well, God can definitely use them to grow our compassion. I would not have chosen to be ill, but now that I have been through that horrible time I am grateful that I am able to empathise with people who are working through their own battles with sickness. I appreciate that I am able to ask helpful questions because I know the questions that helped me, and I love being able to expose lies from the enemy because I know the lies he tried to tell me. It is such a privilege to cry with people when they are waiting for hospital results because I know what that feels like, and to stand with people in faith for supernatural breakthrough when they have lost all hope. People did that for me, and I have learnt that there is always hope when God is in the mix.

About two months after my second surgery, I got to pray for a church leader who was waiting for test results from the hospital. I was keen to pray for him for healing but before I got to that, as I began to connect with how he might be feeling because of my own battles with sickness, I started to pray truth over him. I thanked God that there was no pressure on this leader to walk this path in a particular way, that there was no right or wrong way to model dealing with this to those he was leading, and that it was OK for him to feel disappointed. I thanked God that He was not surprised by the situation, and that He was not worried. I encouraged the leader, and told him that God was really proud of him and really close to him. As a friend and I spoke truth over this leader and his wife, we all cried together and God drew really close and brought incredible comfort, peace and joy.

If you let Him, God will use your own battles and suffering to grow your ability to feel love and compassion for others. Guard against your heart becoming hard because of the pain. Instead, be intentional about praying through the pain or disappointment you have experienced, and allow God to heal your heart. The truth is that what the enemy has meant for harm in your life, God is able to use for good (Genesis 50:20).

3) Ask God to connect your heart to His heart

Growing in love and compassion for others is as simple as asking God to connect your heart to His. This is one of the main ways my heart has grown in love for others. On a fairly consistent basis over the years I have prayed that God would connect my heart to His so that I increasingly feel what He feels. These prayers are usually just one sentence, said either in my head or out loud, whenever I remember I want more compassion.

God has been so faithful in answering my prayers. I now cry fairly regularly with people as they talk to me about the battles they are facing and the suffering they are going through. Every time my heart connects, I thank God for answering my prayers and for the privilege of increasingly loving people like He loves them. God is eager for His children to be motivated by love and moved with compassion as they go after the normal Christian life. Whenever you think about it, ask God to increasingly connect your heart to His and then see what the Father will do.

I have approached much of this chapter from my own experience of being on a journey of my heart connecting with God's love and compassion. Some of you have a different journey to go on because you find it easy to connect with God's love for others. For you, compassion is a real challenge because you feel so deeply and get genuinely overwhelmed when you connect with how God feels. I have friends who feel very deeply who have sometimes talked about wishing they could turn their emotions off. Sadly, this is often what happens. When feelings of compassion get too much, people often seek quick-fix comfort instead of engaging with the pain. In the process, their hearts slowly become distanced from the suffering of people around them. If you can relate to this, your journey involves learning how to stay connected without living in a perpetual state of feeling overwhelmed emotionally. Here are some things you could try.

1) Thank God that you feel so deeply. Emotions are a gift from God and make us more like Him. Thank Him that it is not necessary for you to have lots of prayer to feel compassion for people and the world around you. Try not to go down the route of wishing you were less connected; being connected is the best option, even though it can be more painful.

2) Remember that Jesus is the Saviour of the world, not you. The truth is that Jesus is the answer to sickness and loneliness and oppression and fear... Jesus is the answer to everything! So when you feel compassion for an individual or a situation, feel it with an underlying hope and faith, not hopelessness and despair. Jesus is the answer and there is always hope.

3) Ask God what He wants you to do in response to what you feel. You can avoid being overwhelmed by love and compassion

by finding out the specific responsibility God is giving you in each situation, and leaving the rest to Him. Jesus is responsible for the nations of the world and every individual in them. Our responsibility is to be obedient to the part He is asking us to play. That can be a huge source of comfort to us.

Living a naturally supernatural life is not about going through the motions or ticking an 'evangelism box', neither is it about having a good story to share or seeing a miracle. The normal Christian life is primarily about demonstrating to the people we meet how loved and valued they are, and how kind and compassionate our God is. In the parable of the lost coin, the coin that was lost never lost its value (Luke 15:8–10). The people we meet who are lost have incredible value to God, and we have the privilege of searching them out and revealing the truth to them. When your agenda is to love the person in front of you, you follow in the footsteps of the one who gave everything because He so loved the world. 'For God so loved the world, that he gave his only Son' (John 3:16).

Make a decision today to let the compassion in your heart and the promptings of the Holy Spirit get more attention than the fear that wants to hold you back. How about giving an hour to God this week where you walk around town and see if He stirs your heart with compassion for someone you see. When you are motivated by love you get moved with compassion, and when your action is mixed with faith, anything is possible.

NOTES
[1] Helen Wessel, *The Autobiography of Charles G. Finney, The Life Story of America's Greatest Evangelist In His Own Words* (Bloomington, MN:

Bethany House, 1977), p. 29.

[2] Bob Johnson, *Love Stains* (Redding, CA: Red Arrow Media, 2012) p. 38.

[3] The Father Heart Conference usually takes place in October. For more information about the conference and how to book a ticket, visit www.kingsarms.org.

6
CULTIVATE A LIFESTYLE OF THANKSGIVING

I experienced the power of thanksgiving first-hand during a time of worship at TSM one evening. As the worship started, I was quickly aware of how tired people were around the room. We did not have anyone leading us on a guitar, so it was down to the students and the team to lead themselves into worship. People were singing their own songs to God, and every so often someone shared something from the front, but the overriding atmosphere in the room could only be described as lethargic. That is until one of our students started to shout out a prayer of thanksgiving to God.

It was like something came alive in the student's heart as she declared truth after truth about God's nature. She thanked Him for His goodness and His grace, His love and His kindness. Her prayer of thanksgiving went on and on until she ran out of words to say. 'God, you're just brilliant!' was how her prayer ended. The atmosphere in the room went from being lethargic to electric. The thanksgiving not only made something come alive in the student's heart, it made the rest of us come alive too. One prayer of thanksgiving resulted in a tangible rise of faith across the whole room. It was a powerful moment that had a significant impact on the rest of the evening.

Thanksgiving is powerful, and is a crucial tool in the pursuit of a naturally supernatural life. It often results in a rise of faith because it focuses our attention on who God is and what He is capable of doing. When you remember who God is and all that is possible for Him, you increasingly live with an expectation to see His Kingdom break out wherever you go. Living with a thankful heart and living the normal Christian life go hand in hand. It is very difficult to see God's Kingdom break in on a regular basis if you are not intentional about cultivating a lifestyle of thanksgiving.

Thanksgiving not only raises our faith, it also demonstrates to God how much breakthrough we can be trusted with. I once heard someone say, 'If you cannot celebrate when you see a headache healed you cannot be trusted with an empty wheelchair.' Thanksgiving is key to God entrusting us with greater miracles and signs and wonders. When we are continually thankful for the 'small' things we see God do, He knows we can be trusted with 'bigger' things, because He knows He will get all the glory. Genuine thanksgiving in our hearts opens the door for God's Kingdom to increasingly break out in us and through us. No earthly parent is excited to keep giving good gifts to ungrateful children! God loves it when His kids are thankful.

If it is true that thanksgiving paves the way for God's Kingdom to break in, it is also true that a lack of thanksgiving in our lives may limit what God will do and how He can use us. I did a study once about the Israelites' journey from slavery in Egypt to inheriting the Promised Land. I wanted to learn how almost an entire generation missed out on inheriting the promise God had given them. What mistakes did they make that led to them walking around the desert for forty years, rather than conquering a land flowing with milk and honey? A lack of thanksgiving was a major contributing factor.

The Israelites experienced a whole host of supernatural breakthrough in their escape from Egypt. They witnessed the ten plagues on the Egyptians, they were led by a pillar of cloud by day and a pillar of fire by night, they were led through the Red Sea on dry ground, God provided food and water for them whenever they needed it, and they literally saw God's glory as He spoke with Moses face to face (Exodus 7–33). Instead of these moments of God's miraculous intervention leading to overflowing thankfulness in their hearts, Scripture tells us that the Israelites spent much of their time grumbling about the situation they were in and often wishing they were back in slavery: 'And the whole congregation of the people of Israel grumbled against Moses and Aaron in the wilderness … "Would that we had died by the hand of the LORD in the land of Egypt, when we sat by the meat pots and ate bread to the full, for you have brought us out into this wilderness to kill this whole assembly with hunger"' (Exodus 16:2,3).

There are only two accounts recorded in Scripture, also in Exodus, when the Israelites responded in worship and thanksgiving to God. Once when they first realised God had heard their cries for freedom, and again after they had crossed the Red Sea. Other than these two occasions, thanksgiving was pretty much non-existent. The Israelites' grumbling prevented them from being used by God to see His Kingdom advance on the earth. It was only when almost the entire generation had died that the next generation would take Jericho and get back on track with God's purposes.

When it comes to grumbling, some of us are often not so different from the Israelites. We can experience so much of the goodness of God – His protection, His provision, miracles, freedom, accurate words of knowledge – and yet, like the Israelites, thanksgiving can be scarce. Sometimes this is because we have not worked through pain or disappointment in our hearts; sometimes it is because life has got on top of us and we have lost perspective. A significant part of our journey on TSM and as a church has been learning how to cultivate a lifestyle of thanksgiving and to really celebrate when God breaks in. Having thanksgiving as a default response is key as you learn to live like Jesus. There is still so much for us to learn, but here are some of the lessons God has taught us over the years.

FOCUS ON WHAT GOD *IS* DOING

One of the ways you can cultivate a lifestyle of thanksgiving is by being intentional about focusing your attention on what God is doing, rather than what He has not yet done. In any given situation, you can either choose to focus on what God has done that you can be thankful for and celebrate, or you can focus on what God has not done, which can lead to grumbling and complaining. Where would you say your focus is most of the time? If you are someone like me, you will be easily disappointed when things you are asking God to do have not yet happened. I think for many of us our default thinking is to focus on what God has not yet done, and when this is our focus, thanksgiving can quickly become a very sporadic part of our lives. Choosing to stop thinking about what has not happened and instead focus on what God has done takes discipline.

When I first began stepping out in words of knowledge at our Sunday services, I would bring very general words at the end of the meeting, words about back pain or shoulder pain. Over time, I grew in accuracy as I brought more specific details. At first I got the details wrong, but after a while people started to respond to the more specific words. It was so exciting! The frustrating thing was that although the words of knowledge were now accurate, the people responding to the words were not getting healed when we prayed. For example, I would bring a word about a man who had injured his right knee playing football the previous week and a guy would respond, but when we prayed for him seemingly nothing would happen. I began to get disillusioned and I felt confused.

After one particular service when the same scenario had happened again, I walked out to my car with Simon and asked him why he thought this was happening.[1] I wanted to hear his take on why people were not getting healed, even though our words of knowledge were increasingly accurate. His answer was so helpful. He told me that he could not explain why people were not getting healed, he was just as confused as me about that, but he did encourage me to shift my focus. Simon suggested that I made a decision to spend more time thinking about what was happening, rather than what we were not yet seeing. The fact that I was beginning to hear God with much more accuracy was definitely something to celebrate.

I had been asking God for more specific details when I brought words of knowledge for a while. I wanted to hear His voice with increased accuracy because I wanted people to be overwhelmed by how intimately God knew them. When God started to answer my prayers, I almost missed the opportunity to celebrate and get thankful because my default focus was on what was not yet happening. This timely provocation from Simon changed my mind-set. I started to thank God that I was hearing His voice more accurately and that people were responding to the words of knowledge I was bringing. After this shift in focus, it was not long before we not only had people responding to accurate words of knowledge, they were totally healed as well. My choice to focus on and be thankful for what God was doing was the key that opened the door to more of His power breaking in.[2]

Focusing on what God is doing also helps you to stay thankful as you navigate difficult circumstances that seem to make no sense. In the chapter Know Who God Is, I have already talked about the importance of living unoffended with God when it comes to living the normal Christian life. Staying focused on what God is doing and choosing to thank Him for these things really helps us steer clear of offence. I am not saying we should ignore pain and disappointment. I hope I have already made it clear that expressing pain and working through disappointment is vitally important if you want to live with expectation that God's Kingdom could break in at any moment. What I am saying is that there are always things we can be thankful for no matter what situation we find ourselves in, and it is important that we make a conscious decision to look for these.

A friend of mine lost her battle with breast cancer over the Christmas holiday of 2008. She was an outstanding woman of God and a much-loved and respected member of our church family. We prayed for her consistently throughout her treatment and had believed for a miracle that never came. It was very painful and hugely disappointing. Since her death, we have prayed for several women who have gone on to testify to lumps disappearing from their breasts. The situation is full of mystery, and it would have been so easy for many of us to go down the route of offence. But when I look back at everything that happened, there are so many things I can choose to be thankful for. I am thankful that my friend is now in heaven, pain-free and worshipping the one she was so in love with. I am thankful for all that I learnt from my friend while she was alive and what she taught me about finishing well, with such dignity and unwavering faith. I am thankful that as a church we are beginning to see breast cancer defeated by the power of God. No matter what situation you find yourself in, it is always possible to focus on what God is doing and so be thankful. God loves a thankful heart.

LEARN TO REALLY CELEBRATE

We love to share stories of what God is doing in and through us at our Sunday meetings. Firstly, because we want to get excited about who He is and to celebrate His goodness, but also because we want to raise faith in our church family that what God has done before He wants to do again. Sharing stories of what God is doing is incredibly powerful.

I remember the Sunday we had our first story of a healing that had taken place 'on the streets'. We had seen a lot of healing in the church by this point, and were feeling increasingly convinced that God wanted to use us to see His Kingdom come outside the church in our everyday lives. The problem was, we were so full of fear. To help us grow in courage, we set a goal as a church to see thirty miracles on the streets between 2008 and 2012. When we set the goal we had not seen any, and we were now three months into our allotted time with no success. Then we got one! This was the moment we had been waiting for. Somebody actually got healed outside the four walls of our church. This was an incredibly significant milestone for us as a church family. Little did we know that this particular Sunday would also be the catalyst for teaching us how to properly celebrate when God impacts lives.

I interviewed my friend about his encounter on the train. He had been travelling back to Bedford from Manchester. After exchanging a few pleasantries with the businesswoman sitting next to him, he noticed her reach into her handbag to retrieve some strong-looking tablets. My friend asked the lady what was wrong, and she told him that she was suffering with chronic pain in her neck and that it was keeping her awake at night. My friend knew that this was an opportunity to see God's Kingdom come 'on the streets', but he was wrestling with so much fear. In order to delay offering to pray, he asked the lady if she was having treatment. She said she was, but that it was not working. With nowhere else to go, my friend mustered up all the courage he could and asked the lady if she would let him pray for her. To his surprise she accepted. After a short and slightly awkward prayer all the pain in this lady's neck had gone. This now bewildered lady experienced the healing power of God on a train! This is what we had been waiting for. We had got our first miracle on the street!

When my friend finished sharing his story, we responded as a church in the same way we always did when interviews finished, with a polite and subdued applause. Simon decided to do something entirely different. As the interview finished he jumped to his feet and celebrated with whooping and shouts of 'JESUS!'. I remember the moment so clearly. All of us turned to look at him mid-clap, not sure whether we too should jump to our feet or stay as we were. It was pretty awkward for a moment, but Simon's willingness to break the mould turned out to be a major turning point for us as a church.

We now realise that our response to what God was doing had been totally inappropriate. We were regularly hearing stories about God's Kingdom advancing in amazing ways. Stories of people healed and set free and transformed as they gave their lives to Jesus. Yet every time we responded as a church with what we now refer to as golf claps. Polite and automatic applause, appropriate for a golf course but totally inappropriate for stories of God's Kingdom coming. We have since learnt that we need to be much more like our heavenly Father when it comes to celebrating lives transformed.

When Jesus tells the parable of the prodigal son, His description of the Father shows us how to celebrate appropriately when God's Kingdom advances: be emotionally involved, be expressive, make some noise, be extravagant and over the top and throw a party (Luke 15:11–32). We have made a decision as a church that when it comes to responding to God's goodness, there are no golf claps allowed. Now when stories are shared on a Sunday about God's Kingdom coming, it is very common to hear shouts and cheers and loud applause all across the room. Anything less is an inappropriate response to the kindness and grace of God. Learning to really celebrate in a way that involves your heart and your body, not just your head and your hands, is key to seeing sustained outbreaks of God's power. By the end of 2008 we had seen around seventy miracles 'on the streets', more than double what we were aiming for over five years. I think our newfound celebration was a key reason for this. How well are you celebrating when you hear stories of God's Kingdom breaking in?

It is important that we also learn to celebrate when others get the breakthrough we are longing for. In these times the cost of our celebration goes to a whole new level, but then, so does our relationship with God. Often it is our ability to celebrate when someone else gets the breakthrough we want that provides the platform for our own breakthrough.

I learnt this the hard way when we first started the process of taking the Kingdom of God onto the streets. I had read the book *The Ultimate Treasure Hunt* and had written some training for people who were interested to learn what treasure hunting was all about.[3] I had taken a few teams out and we had seen some clues begin to match up, but not much else in the way of healing or salvation. I was desperate to see extraordinary miracles outside the church, the kind of breakthroughs that were commonplace in Acts.

A few months after this whole process began, Simon went into the town with a friend for what was probably his third treasure hunt. Seven teenagers were healed in one hit during this street encounter![4] Simon and his friend saw God's kingdom break out on the streets in ways we had only ever dreamed of before. A teenage guy with a chronic back condition was pain-free, a girl who had a broken arm was able to move it without pain, and someone who was short-sighted began to read things they could not have read before. Miracles were taking place with unforeseen ease. At one point during the encounter Simon shouted out to people to come over if they needed healing because God was doing miracles. This was in the town centre in Bedford! Their time together finished with Simon giving the gospel to those who had gathered.

Later that evening, when I heard what had happened, on the outside I was really excited but on the inside it was a different story. On the outside I celebrated what God had done along with everyone else, but on the inside my heart was hard and jealous and annoyed. This was not fair! I had been out on the streets loads more than Simon. I was the one who had read the book and written the training. Simon had the breakthrough I was longing for, and what it exposed in my heart was ugly. The amount of Kingdom activity I saw in the season following slowed down a bit until I was able to really celebrate what God had done, and that he had done it through Simon. I came to realise pretty quickly that it was God's goodness that Simon had this encounter. When a church leader gets hold of something it naturally impacts the rest of the church. Since that time, I have learnt the significance of really celebrating when other people get the breakthrough I am longing for. It not only deepens my relationship with God, it reminds me that living a supernatural life is not about me, but all about Him and His glory.

GUARD AGAINST OVERFAMILIARITY

Any breakthrough we have the privilege of being part of, whether we consider it to be big or small, is significant and worth getting excited about. I have had to regularly remind myself of this on my journey of longing for more of God's Kingdom. I remember the season when it was commonplace for us to see backs healed at King's Arms. Almost every week at church backs would get healed, and out on the streets the story was the same. I remember walking past a lady one Sunday on my way to the bathroom, and putting my hand on her back to say hello. She commented on the fact that my hand was hot, and I made a throwaway comment about it being because I was called to heal the sick. Before I could walk any further, she grabbed my hand and put it on her back again, asking me to pray. She explained that her back was bad and that she was in a lot of pain. After a very simple prayer, all the pain in her back had totally gone. She spent the rest of the meeting crouched over doing kids' work, completely pain-free. That is how easy it was. After a while, I began to lose thanksgiving in my heart for the healing we were seeing. We had done backs, now I wanted to move on to more 'impressive' miracles.

I have learnt over the years that any time I stop being thankful for what God is doing in people's lives, my celebration has become about me. My celebration has become about whether I feel like I am growing in my ability to see miracles, rather than how amazing God is or the fact that yet another person has experienced life change. I lost my ability to celebrate backs being healed because I lost sight of the fact that every back healed meant that someone else was now pain-free and able to do things they could not do before. I lost sight of the fact that every healing represented the goodness and grace of God being poured into an individual's life, and that the only appropriate response was to really celebrate because God had done it again. I lost sight of the fact that the healing breakthroughs were not about me, but were about Him and His glory. I had fallen into the snare of overfamiliarity.

Overfamiliarity is a major roadblock if you want to go after a naturally supernatural life. It robs you of thanksgiving and stops you really celebrating, and it needs to be avoided at all costs. Overfamiliarity is a particular danger when living a supernatural life becomes increasingly natural. At TSM, we share stories most weeks of encounters we have had on the streets, and how we have seen God break in during our everyday lives. I remember one Thursday we had thirty minutes of stories, which was not uncommon, but these stories were particularly exciting. I forget all the details of what was shared, but I remember feeling something new was happening.

It felt like we were seeing more significant outbreaks of God's Kingdom with greater ease. We celebrated in the same way we always did as each story was shared, loudly and with lots of cheers, and then I left the room to go to a meeting.

As I walked out of the TSM room, the Holy Spirit nudged me. I knew in my heart that we had not celebrated enough in response to the incredible stories that had been shared. We were suddenly seeing things we had only dreamed about a few months earlier, and yet our celebration was unaffected. We had become overfamiliar in our hearts with God's Kingdom advancing because we heard so many stories, week in and week out. Our celebration was usually loud and exuberant, but the Holy Spirit's provocation exposed that even exuberant celebration can sometimes become a habit rather than a response to genuine thanksgiving in our hearts.

When I returned to TSM to speak in the second session, I started by sharing what the Holy Spirit had shown me. I reminded the students that several years ago we were seeing almost nothing as a church, hardly any healing breakthroughs and certainly no accurate words of knowledge. I reminded them that hearing stories every week of lives being impacted by God was something we only dreamed of, and now it was happening! Before I spoke, we took some time to really celebrate what God had done that week, from the heart. It was another turning point for us.

I remember being at a conference and listening to a well-known international speaker who has seen thousands of miracles over the course of many years as a result of his ministry. If anyone could be in danger of becoming overfamiliar with miracles, it would be him. Yet every time a testimony of healing was shared, celebration just flowed out of his heart. He punched the air, thanked God out loud, welled up with emotion, and at one point told us that a testimony had given him goose bumps. God is looking for hearts He can trust with increased breakthrough. He is looking for hearts that celebrate again and again as backs and shoulders and legs and headaches are healed, and as cancers and incurable diseases bow the knee to His name. All are miraculous, all are amazing, and all require celebration. God loves it when His kids are thankful.

THE POWER OF THANKSGIVING

What amazes me is that thanksgiving in and of itself is powerful enough to transform circumstances and advance God's Kingdom. Contrast for a minute the response of the Israelites when they were brought out of slavery with the response of Paul and Silas when they were put in prison for preaching the gospel:

> Around midnight Paul and Silas were praying and singing hymns to God, and the other prisoners were listening. Suddenly, there was a massive earthquake, and the prison was shaken to its foundations. All the doors immediately flew open, and the chains of every prisoner fell off! The jailer woke up to see the prison doors wide open. He assumed the prisoners had escaped, so he drew his sword to kill himself. But Paul shouted to him, 'Stop! Don't kill yourself! We are all here!'
>
> The jailer called for lights and ran to the dungeon and fell down trembling before Paul and Silas. Then he brought them out and asked, 'Sirs, what must I do to be saved?'
>
> They replied, 'Believe in the Lord Jesus and you will be

saved, along with everyone in your household.' And they shared the word of the Lord with him and with all who lived in his household. Even at that hour of the night, the jailer cared for them and washed their wounds. Then he and everyone in his household were immediately baptized. He brought them into his house and set a meal before them, and he and his entire household rejoiced because they all believed in God. (Acts 16:25–34, NLT)

The Israelites were set free from the debilitating oppression of the Egyptians, but their primary response was to grumble. The result of their grumbling was that they did not inherit the incredible promises God had prepared for them. Paul and Silas were put in prison following a severe beating with rods from the crowds. Their freedom was taken away from them, but their response was to worship. The result of their worship was a supernatural prison break, which led to the jailor and his entire household giving their lives to Jesus. Paul and Silas' worship resulted in the Kingdom of God advancing. We must not underestimate the power of thanksgiving in our lives.

The Kingdom of God is forcefully advancing: lives are being saved; bodies and hearts are being healed and set free; people are experiencing peace and joy and justice; and towns, cities and nations are being transformed by the love of God. We are seeing things now that we only dreamed of seeing a few years ago. God is looking for sons and daughters who will focus on what He is doing and cultivate a lifestyle of thanksgiving. He is looking for individuals and churches that know what it is to really celebrate when His Kingdom advances. Celebration that is not inhibited by overfamiliarity or the fear of what those around us might think; celebration that overflows from the heart and is expressive.

Why not decide today that next time you hear a story of God's Kingdom breaking in, you give yourself permission to really celebrate? What would that look like for you? Thanksgiving is a powerful weapon when it comes to living a naturally supernatural life. God loves to entrust more of His Kingdom to thankful hearts.

NOTES

[1] Simon Holley is Lead Elder at King's Arms and is author of the book *Sustainable Power: Creating a Healthy Culture of the Supernatural in the Church Today* (Milton Keynes: Authentic Media, 2013).

[2] We have found words of knowledge to be a great way of raising corporate faith on Sundays. When we started out learning to hear God's voice, Simon and I would get words of knowledge wrong all the time. As people have seen us continue to take risks and grow in our ability to hear God accurately, many others in the church have been mobilised. The truth is that everybody can grow in hearing God's voice with increased accuracy.

[3] Kevin Dedmon, *The Ultimate Treasure Hunt* (Shippensburg, PA: Destiny Image Publishers, 2007).

[4] You can watch the full story on our website:
www.kingsarms.org/resources/media/message/seven-teenagers-healed.html.

7
MAKE A PLAN
TO REMEMBER

Remembering and thanksgiving should be two sides of the same coin. When you remember who God is and what He has done you get thankful, and when you make a conscious decision to practise thanksgiving, it helps you to remember. Remembering is a key principle when it comes to pursuing a naturally supernatural life. It helps us approach 'impossible' situations from a place of faith rather than unbelief. When we remember who God is, that at the core of His being He is loving and kind and good, we get convinced that He wants to break in with His love, kindness and goodness in every situation we find ourselves in. When we remember what God has done before, like breakthroughs in healing and salvation and freedom and provision and accurate words of knowledge (I could go on), it shows us the things He wants to do again. I have dedicated a whole chapter to the subject of remembering, because it is so easy for us to forget who God is and what He loves to do.

My study of the Israelites showed how linked thanksgiving and remembering really is. The Israelites' grumbling meant they forgot what God was like and what He had done for them, and their failure to remember added more fuel to their grumbling. The Israelites' inability to remember contributed just as a much to them not inheriting the Promised Land as their lack of thanksgiving. It would be easy for us to read about the Israelites and judge them for their failures. How could they get it so wrong? We put ourselves in their shoes and think that if we ever walked through a sea on dry ground we would never grumble, because who experiences that kind of miracle and wishes they could go back into slavery? We think we would always remember what God had done and what He is like, because whoever forgets when they are led by a pillar of cloud and fire?

Before we get too judgemental of the Israelites, we have to remember that they had been taken out of a place that had become very familiar to them, and taken into the unknown. They had a promise from God, but a man they did not know had delivered it to them. They were then led by this man without knowing any details about how they would eat, where they would get water, where they would sleep, how safe they would be, or where they would ultimately end up. In addition to this, there was the reality of their daily struggle of being in a harsh and barren dessert. We assume that anything would be better than slavery, but think for a minute how you feel when God leads you into unfamiliar territory, where it feels scary and uncertain and you have no idea of the plan. Like when you have no idea where your finances will come from, or when you are waiting to hear if your treatment at the hospital has worked, or when God prompts you to pray for a stranger on the streets. In times like this, it can be difficult to remember who God is and how faithful He has been to us in the past. As I have said before, we are often not so different from the Israelites!

When Moses handed the baton to Joshua, he had stern

words for the Israelites who would finally inherit the Promised Land. He was well aware that the previous generation's inability to remember who God was and what He had done was a key reason they missed out on their inheritance. He did not want this generation to make the same mistake, and so he repeatedly urged the Israelites to remember, for example:

> Only take care, and keep your soul diligently, lest you forget the things that your eyes have seen, and lest they depart from your heart all the days of your life. Make them known to your children and your children's children … (Deuteronomy 4:9)

> Take care, lest you forget the covenant of the LORD your God, which he made with you, and make a carved image, the form of anything that the LORD your God has forbidden you. (Deuteronomy 4:23)

Moses emphasised the importance of remembering time and time again because he knew how easy it would be for the Israelites to forget.

IT IS SO EASY TO FORGET

During the Sunday of our TSM graduation service in 2013, God's Kingdom broke out in incredible ways throughout the course of the day. Let me summarise some of what happened:

1) When I had finished preaching, one of our TSM students brought her first-ever word of knowledge from the front. She had the name Marie and a sense that God was speaking about forgiveness, either the need to forgive or be forgiven.

A lady approached her at the end of the meeting to respond. This lady's sister was called Marie and they had only spoken two or three times in the last twenty-five years. She had been speaking with some of her family just the day before about needing to forgive her sister. God spoke into the situation the very next day! Our student was able to lead this lady through a process of forgiving her sister. Not bad for your first-ever word of knowledge!

2) Another of our students had a word of knowledge about someone with metal somewhere in the right side of their body. She got to pray for a man who had metal in his right forearm as a result of a motorbike accident. His arm had been incredibly stiff that week, due to starting a new job which involved a lot of lifting. After they prayed, the man testified to his arm being significantly looser and the ridge he could usually feel when pressing along his scar had gone. When I emailed him the following week, he told me that his arm was 'the loosest it has been for over thirty-five years'.

3) In the afternoon, one of our TSM team realised he had lost his keys. He thought they may have dropped out in someone's car earlier in the day, but when he asked them to check there was no sign of them. He had heard a story of a friend whose bankcard got stuck in an ATM machine, but how after she prayed, God miraculously put the card back in her purse. So he prayed, confessing to God that he was not sure he actually had faith for anything to happen, but asking if he could have his keys back. Later in the evening, he got a call from a friend who had just got home and got his keys out to open his front door. The entire set of keys that had been lost was attached to his house keys, and he could think of no explanation!

4) In the evening, we were running an event to raise money

for our young people to go to Newday, a major youth camping event that takes place every summer. During the rehearsals, three young men walked into our church building and got chatting to one of the youth leaders. It turns out that they had met some of our TSM students on the streets a few weeks earlier, and they had decided to come and find out what the church was all about. After a short conversation and some prayer, the youth leader got to lead one of the guys to the Lord. What I love about this story is that this man gave his life to Jesus during a youth event rehearsal, not our usual church service. God is mighty to save!

I am telling you these stories firstly just because they are amazing and need to be celebrated. God's goodness is relentless. But secondly, to illustrate how easy it is to forget what God is like. I woke up on the Monday after this day full of miracles feeling miserable and questioning God's goodness. I was feeling particularly frustrated about being single and not having kids; about my life not looking how I dreamed it would when I was little. I was questioning whether God really cared about me and whether He really did have good plans for my life. To be honest, I was grumbling like the Israelites. (I have worked through disappointment about being single and not having children on many occasions, which is really important to do. If we are honest with ourselves, I think we can usually tell the difference between processing disappointment and just having a grumble. If we are not sure in the moment, it is great to have friends who can help us work it out!)

As I shared what I was feeling with a friend, God began to bring to my mind all that He had done the day before. My friend and I retold the stories to each other and, as we did, thanksgiving and faith began to rise up in my heart. I made a note of the many ways God had broken in on my phone so I could remember, and we celebrated the astounding breakthroughs. Being intentional about remembering what God had done meant I remembered what He is like. I remembered that He is always good and always kind, and that His plans for my life are the best.

When we forget what God does, we forget what He is like, and unbelief can settle in our hearts. It is so important that we make a plan to remember. When you are used by God to see His Kingdom advance, you think you will never forget what happened, but in my experience we remember very little if we are not intentional about remembering. Remembering enables us to approach opportunities to see God's Kingdom break in from a place of faith. When we remember what God has done in the past, faith gets fuelled in our hearts because we know that what God has done before demonstrates what He wants to do again. Remembering enables us to pursue a naturally supernatural life with expectation.

I have already told you about the toddler I met at the hospital who fell asleep about thirty seconds after I prayed for him for peace. Fast forward a few years and I was outside the hospital again, this time talking to a lady suffering with schizophrenia. As we talked, I remembered what had happened when I prayed for the toddler and faith began to rise in my heart. I knew that if this lady agreed to let us pray for her she would receive God's peace, and the turmoil she was experiencing in her mind would be stilled. After offering three times to pray, she agreed. I simply held her hand and asked the Prince of Peace to come and meet with his daughter, and He did. With a big smile on her face she quizzed us about was going on.

She told us that she suddenly felt so much peace. It was such a privilege to see God's Kingdom break into this woman's life. The key to being so convinced God was going to break in when we prayed was remembering what He had done before.

MAKE A PLAN

In order to remember, we need to be intentional about making a plan. Here are some ways we can intentionally remember who God is and what He loves to do.

1) Read the Bible

Scripture shows us what God is like. It teaches us what God loves and what He hates. It shows us His heart and His nature and the things He loves to do. The Gospels are great books to study to discover God's passion about His Kingdom breaking out in everyday life. '[Jesus] is the radiance of the glory of God and the exact imprint of his nature' (Hebrews 1:3). If you want to know what God feels about sickness, look at Jesus' response to it. If you want to know if God is passionate about people getting free, look at how Jesus deals with oppression. If you want to know how God feels about His Kingdom, read Jesus' teaching and look at how He spent His time.

It is so important that we do not reduce what the Bible teaches to fit in with our experience. Healing was a huge part of Jesus' ministry on the earth. If people are not healed when we pray for them, we cannot conclude that God is indifferent about sickness or that He does not want to use us. Instead, we must cry out to God for more breakthroughs so that our experience would increasingly line up with what Jesus modelled for us in the Gospels. Jesus tells us that the harvest is plentiful, that there are lots of people ready to give their lives to Him. If we have never led someone to Jesus, or it has been a long time since we have seen someone saved in our church, we must not conclude that the gospel is not as powerful as Scripture makes it out to be. Instead, we must call out to Jesus, the Lord of the harvest, to save our friends and family and work colleagues and those we meet on the streets.

The truth is that God is incredibly passionate about His Kingdom breaking out on the earth. He is eager for the sick to be healed, the broken to be bound up, the oppressed to be set free, and those who are lost to come into relationship with Him. The truth is that when we study Scripture and spend time meditating on the life of Jesus, we remember why He came and we remember what He has commissioned us to do. We remember that we are anointed to see the Kingdom of God break out wherever we see the kingdom of darkness at work. And when we remember, we live with expectation that God wants to use us to reveal Jesus wherever we go.

2) Read biographies about heroes of the faith

I love reading biographies about men and women who have been used by God to see Kingdom outbreak and revival. They stir my faith and provoke me to ask God for more. When you read stories of what God has done in the past through men and women like you and me, it shows you what is possible again. The stories we read are often so far removed from what we have experienced, but they are not meant to frustrate or depress us. Rather, they are meant to encourage us to expect greater things from the God who never changes and whose Kingdom is always advancing.

If we read about Kathryn Kuhlman's incredible dependence on the Holy Spirit and the innumerable miracles and salvations that resulted, we can be encouraged to pray for more of God's presence in our lives.

If we read about how the glory of God invaded the Azusa Street revival so much that flames of fire were seen on top of the building where they met, we can long for more of God's glory, His tangible presence, invading our churches.

If we read about Charles Finney's love for those who were lost and his passion to see them saved, we can be challenged to ask God for increased compassion in our hearts for the lost and broken we come into contact with every day.

If we read about the thousands of orphans looked after in Mozambique, and the multitude of provision and healing miracles Heidi and Rolland Baker have seen as they have said yes to God, we can be provoked to pursue a lifestyle of radical obedience.[1]

Biographies are faith-building and exciting and challenging, but most of all they remind us who God is and what He loves to do through normal men and women who choose to say yes to Him. Have you got a biography on the go?

3) Get thankful

The previous chapter is all about the importance of thanksgiving as you seek to live the life that Jesus lived, so just a little reminder here. Prioritising thanksgiving in our lives helps us to remember who God is and what He is like. Thanksgiving also reminds us what God loves to do, and keeps these things alive in our hearts. Thanksgiving is a powerful tool in the process of remembering. Be intentional about making it a discipline in your life.

4) Find a way of recording what God does in and through you

When you are in the midst of an encounter where God's Kingdom is breaking in, you think you will never forget what God did and how He used you. Seeing someone healed for the first time; leading someone to Jesus on the streets; bringing a word of knowledge that is really accurate; prophesying over someone in a coffee shop: these are all defining milestones as you learn to live a naturally supernatural life. I have found that it is really easy to forget what God does, unless you have a plan for recording your stories.

When I first started on this journey, I decided to write a blog. I had no idea what I was doing and had never written before, but it was an easy way of being intentional about recording stories. Now I tend to keep notes on my phone or use Twitter or Facebook to record breakthroughs I have seen or heard about.[2] It is always such an encouragement to reread stories of breakthrough, and my faith is always stirred as a result. What often surprises me is how much of the journey and how many of the stories I have forgotten. Work out a way of recording what God does in and through you, and then carve out time to start recording some stories.

5) Be a storyteller

The stories we tell at King's Arms are a great way to remember what God has done, and they help to raise corporate faith. In addition to upfront stories, we encourage each individual to become a story magnet when it comes to Kingdom outbreak. I remember having lunch with some friends of mine who are all hungry for more of God and more of His Kingdom invading the earth. We spent most of our time together sharing stories of what we had heard or seen God do over the last few months;

we were literally tripping over each other to share. There were stories of miraculous provision, gospel conversations with Muslims, a lady miraculously healed from cancer, a lady coming out of a coma after prayer, and many more. The faith in the room as story after story was shared was tangible.

Make a decision to be a storyteller. Avoid exaggerating stories to make them sound better or downplaying what God has done. When you share stories authentically, it helps people who are naturally cynical or sceptical. Start your family meal times with stories of God's goodness; at church meetings or when you meet together in smaller groups, share stories of God's Kingdom coming; make time when you hang out with friends to talk about what God has done in and through you, and to share stories you have heard from other people. And when you share stories, remember to get really thankful and really celebrate the goodness and grace of God. It is all about Him and all because of Him and all for Him.

IMPACTING FUTURE GENERATIONS

Making a plan to remember is crucial for us as individuals as we aim to share Jesus' love with everyone we meet, but it is also crucial for the generations to come. If we want the generations that come after us to step into all we have experienced in God and inherit for free what we have paid a price for, we need to be able to tell them what they are inheriting. We need to be able to tell them stories we have had the privilege of being part of, stories of healing and miracles and lives transformed and communities impacted. We need to have something tangible to pass on to them so that they can expect a naturally supernatural life to be the norm for them.

When Joshua took over leadership of the Israelites to lead

them into the Promised Land, he would have had Moses' instructions to prioritise remembering who God was and what He had done ringing in his ears. After the entire nation of Israel had made their way across the Jordan, God had some very specific instructions for Joshua:

'Take twelve men from the people, from each tribe a man, and command them, saying, "Take twelve stones from here out of the midst of the Jordan, from the very place where the priests' feet stood firmly, and bring them over with you and lay them down in the place where you lodge tonight." Then Joshua called the twelve men from the people of Israel, whom he has appointed, a man from each tribe. … '… When your children ask in time to come, "What do these stones mean to you?" then you shall tell them that the waters of the Jordan were cut off before the ark of the covenant of the LORD. When it passed over the Jordan, the waters of the Jordan were cut off. *So these stones shall be to the people of Israel a memorial for ever*' (Joshua 4:2–7, italics mine).

Each tribe was to be involved in setting up a memorial for the Israelites to remember what God did the day they crossed the Jordan. The memorial was to be for their benefit, but also for the benefit of the generations to come. When the Israelites' children saw the stones and asked what they meant, their parents would tell them of the time God made it possible for their nation to cross the Jordan on dry ground so they could conquer Jericho. As the event was remembered and the story shared, the next generation would be drafted in to the Israelites' inheritance. The victory of the parents would become the victory of the child. The child would get for free what the parents had to pay a price for, and would be fast-tracked in their relationship with God: 'My God is a God of the impossible!'

We have seen this principle of remembering and inheritance take place on TSM as each year has transitioned. During our first year, we saw a number of significant breakthroughs. People were healed on the streets and we saw one person give their life to Jesus. We got permission from the council to set up chairs and a banner in the town centre to pray for people, and we began to learn how to prophesy over members of the public. At the start of each subsequent year, we share with our new students the key memorial stones of what God has done in previous years. This sets the scene for the students and shows them the inheritance that they get to step into for free. They are then able to build on the foundation of previous students' breakthroughs and pay their own price to take things further. With every succeeding TSM year, the momentum that is established through remembering leads to an increase in the number and scale of life-changing encounters on the streets.

Over the years, we have seen many people experience God's love as we have intentionally done outreach. Many people have been healed, and some have responded to the gospel. (Sadly, I do not have exact numbers of people who have said yes to Jesus, because I have not always been intentional enough about remembering. Kind of proves my point that making a plan to remember is important!) We have increasingly been given permission from the council to set up 'stations' in the town centre where we offer to pray for the sick and prophesy over members of the public. On one occasion, the prophetic word some of our students shared with a guy led to him coming to church and recommitting his life to Jesus. We have pioneered different ways of using creativity to share

God's heart with people and to bless businesses. Some of our students drew prophetic pictures for members of the public and then talked through with them what they felt God was saying. We are seeing so much now that we would not have dreamed of seeing when TSM first started. I believe much of the momentum we enjoy is to do with how intentional we are about remembering.

When we remember who God is and what He has done, not only is our faith stirred for greater breakthrough, we also get to pass the baton of our successes to the next generation. As we learn to live like Jesus did, remembering will ensure that momentum is maintained in the midst of all the mystery. When it seems like God is silent or that He is using everyone else but you, remembering will mean that you choose to keep saying yes to Him when opportunities come to see His Kingdom break in. Not only that, remembering will ensure that generations to come will grow up realising that the life Jesus modelled is the normal Christian life for every believer.

Think about whether you already have memorial stones in your life or as a church when it comes to being naturally supernatural. How will you intentionally remember them? If you are right at the beginning of your journey, what would you like your first memorial stone to be? It is time to make a plan to remember.

NOTES

[1] Jamie Buckingham, *Daughter of Destiny* (Alachua, FL: Bridge-Logos, 1999); J. Edward Morris and Cindy McCowan, *Azusa Street: They Told Me Their Stories* (Manhattan, NY: Dare2Dream, 2006); Helen Wessel, *The Autobiography of Charles G. Finney* (Bloomington, MN: Bethany House, 1977); Rolland and Heidi Baker, *Always Enough* (Ada, MI: Chosen Books, 2003).

[2] You can read my blog here wendymann-life.blogspot.com and follow me on Twitter @WendyMann5.

8
TAKE SOME
RISKS

A friend of mine felt prompted by God to buy a bouquet of flowers for one of her colleagues at work. She knew the lady a little bit but not well, and they did not see each other very often. As my friend pulled up at the supermarket, she asked the Holy Spirit if there was any more specific information He wanted to give her. She felt Him say that the flowers should be yellow and that they would cost £20. When my friend looked at the flowers available, the biggest bouquet of yellow flowers cost £18. Thinking that she had heard the cost information wrong, she took the flowers to the checkout, where she was asked if she wanted them specially wrapped for an extra two pounds. Of course, she agreed. When she got back to her car she wrote a gift card to accompany the flowers, detailing three things she felt the Holy Spirit say her colleague really needed to hear.

When my friend got to work, she left the flowers in her car and nervously went into the office. The lady God had spoken to her about was there, so my friend sat at an empty desk pretending to work while she planned her next move. A few minutes later, the lady got up to leave. My friend followed her out of the office, and plucked up as much courage as she could to start up a conversation. She told the lady that she had something for her, and asked if she could wait until she went to get it from her car. The lady looked a bit baffled, but agreed to meet my friend in the car park.

As the lady saw my friend approaching with the bouquet, she started to cry. My friend explained how God had prompted her to buy the flowers for her, and that He had three things He specifically wanted to say to her that were written in the card. The lady could not believe what was happening.

'Do you know? Do you know what's happening? This is amazing! You really don't know?' she repeated disbelievingly.

My friend was completely in the dark, and had no idea why the flowers and what God said in the card meant so much to the lady. She was just grateful that her obedience and the risk she had taken had so obviously blessed her colleague. Later that day, my friend's colleague called her to explain why the gift had been so significant.

This lady was going through a very difficult time. She had found out that weekend that she was pregnant, but her partner was furious. He told her that if she kept the baby she would never see him again, so she booked an abortion for the following week, even though she felt really uncomfortable about it. For the first time in her life this desperate lady had prayed, asking God to give her a sign if He was real and wanted her to keep the baby. She believed that the flowers were that sign. There were two specific fears that the lady had about having the baby on her own, but the Holy Spirit-inspired writing in the gift card addressed both of these and brought peace. This brave lady cancelled the abortion a few days later. Very sadly she had a miscarriage the following week, but the fact that God engaged with her right at the time she needed

Him the most blew both her and my friend away. You just never know how your obedience and the risks you take will change lives.

It is difficult to live a naturally supernatural life without stepping out of your comfort zone and taking some risks. It is great to hear stories of how God's Kingdom is breaking in through other people, and to get convinced from Scripture that He wants to do the same things through us. It is really helpful to listen to training about how to approach people on the streets, and to read books like this that outline important keys for doing the things that Jesus did. Yet there comes a point when you just have to make a conscious decision to push through the fear barrier and have a go. The more risks you take, the more you learn to stop listening to fear and instead tune into the subtle promptings of the Holy Spirit. The more risks you take the more miracles you see, the more you grow in your ability to accurately hear God's voice, and the more you see God's Kingdom break out wherever you go.

Scripture is full of stories of people who took risks in response to God's promptings. In Acts alone the disciples are taking risks all the time. Immediately after Peter and John were released from custody, they gathered with the other apostles and prayed that God would give them increased boldness to preach about Jesus. This was the very thing that had got them arrested in the first place (Acts 4). The disciple Ananias responded to a word of knowledge from God to go and pray for Saul, even though he knew Saul had been persecuting and killing Christians (Acts 9). Peter responded to a vision from God instructing him to go and speak to Gentiles, even though it was unlawful for him to associate with or visit anyone of another nation (Acts 10). The outcome of these risks was a rapid expansion of God's Kingdom.

You cannot know if a word of knowledge you have for someone is right unless you share it with them. You cannot know if someone will get healed if you pray for them unless you pray. You cannot know if someone is ready to give their life to Jesus unless you ask them the question. I hate this and love it all at the same time. I hate it because having to take risks is awkward and uncomfortable and continually exposes how much fear is still lingering in my heart. The fear is so much less than it used to be, but it is definitely still there and I wonder if it always will be. Living a naturally supernatural life is not comfortable. But I love it because having to take risks forces me to be continually dependent on God, which deepens my relationship with Him. It reminds me of my weakness and His strength, and it ensures that God gets all the glory when His Kingdom advances through me. God loves it when we are dependent on Him.

EMBARRASSMENT VERSUS BREAKTHROUGH

When you take risks for God, there are times when you see incredible breakthrough in people's lives. One of our TSM students had an amazing encounter with some teenagers when he was out walking his dog one evening. He passed the teenagers in a park and had a moment of feeling prompted by God to speak to them. He ignored the prod for a while, after all it was dark and this was all new to him, but in the end he decided to be obedient to the Holy Spirit and take a risk. Over the course of his time with these teenagers, all five of them agreed to let him pray with them and each of them felt God's presence. After more conversation, the student felt prompted to ask the teenagers if any of them wanted to give their lives to

Jesus. All five of them said yes! They stood in a circle together holding hands and our student led them in a prayer to come into a relationship with their heavenly Father.

When you take risks for God, there are also times when you get things wrong: when things do not go the way you hoped they would; when people are not interested in being prayed for and it feels like nothing is happening. One of the inevitable outcomes of taking risks is that sometimes things will not go to plan. As you pray for people to be healed and prophesy over strangers, there will be plenty of opportunities to be discouraged and give up and stop taking risks. Those who keep saying yes to Jesus over the long haul have generally learnt to navigate mistakes and discouragements well.

I remember a mistake I made when I went with a friend to prophesy over people in a church he had been invited to preach at. I had not been a Christian long and had only prophesied a few times before. I remember being completely terrified as I paced up and down at the back of the hall pleading with God to speak to me as the rest of the congregation worshipped. I was desperate to have a prophetic word to bring so that I would not look like a fool when my friend invited me up to the front. To my great relief, God began to speak to me about a teenage girl sitting on the back row: about how priceless she was to Him. He wanted her to know how loved she was.

When it was my turn to prophesy I encouraged the girl to stand so that I could share what I felt God wanted to say. Unfortunately, my nerves got the better of me and my words came out wrong. I ended up telling the girl, in front of the whole congregation, that God wanted her to know that she was really worthless! It was only seconds before I realised what I had said and was able to rectify the situation, communicating what God had actually said. To say I was a bit embarrassed about what happened would be an understatement. I had taken a risk and it had resulted in a very humiliating mistake. It would have been easy for me to give in to discouragement and make a decision to never prophesy again.

When you take a risk and it all goes wrong, there are always two ways you can respond. You can stop taking risks in the area that brought you the embarrassment. The trouble with this is that you will struggle to grow in your relationship with God and you may limit what He wants to do through you. Alternatively, you can get up, brush yourself off and choose to have another go, to take another risk. I am so glad I chose the second option after my terrible experience. I have brought many prophetic words and words of knowledge from the front of church and out on the streets since that time. I have made lots more mistakes along the way, but I have also had the privilege of seeing many people encountering the love of God as I have shared His heart with them.

One particular time stands out to me. It was a Sunday morning and the plan was to prophesy over people from the front at the end of the service. I asked God to speak to me about a young man I had never met before, sitting a few rows behind me. I saw a picture of him kicking a rugby ball and then immediately holding his back. I felt God speak to me about this man suffering with a back injury that was causing him pain. At the end of the meeting, I picked the guy out and asked him if he played rugby. He told me he had not played a game since he was a kid. It would have been easy for me to give up at that point and assume that I had heard God wrong, but I decided to take another risk and ask him if he had anything wrong with his back. Immediately, his girlfriend put her hand to her mouth and began to cry. After a conversation with them later, I understood why.

This man suffered from a serious back injury. He and his girlfriend worked for a church nearby, but happened to have that morning off. They were desperate for an end to his debilitating pain, and so had done a Google search that morning of 'Backs healed in Bedford'. A story on our church website was the top hit on the page, so they found out where we met and how to get to us. This discouraged guy had come along to King's Arms specifically to get his back prayed for, but even before he had the chance to ask for prayer, God had picked him out through my word of knowledge!

The young man experienced some relief from the pain in his back but he did not leave totally healed, which was a bit of a mystery. He did, however, experience some emotional healing. He told me that he had come to church that morning in a really low place. He had been questioning if God really heard his prayers or if He actually cared about his situation. My word of knowledge silenced the doubts this guy was having, and convinced Him that God did know him and that He was really close.

RELEASED TO MAKE MISTAKES

In order to do the things that Jesus did, you have to be willing to take some risks, and in order to be willing to take risks, you have to be OK with making mistakes. Making mistakes is one of the best ways to learn how to recognise opportunities to see God's Kingdom come and to grow in your ability to hear God's voice. I am learning not to be discouraged when I make mistakes but to enjoy the journey of walking through fear and taking risks. Two key revelations have really helped me over the years to keep responding to promptings from the Holy Spirit, especially when things go wrong.

1) Realise your identity in Christ is nothing to do with your performance

Jesus received His identity as the beloved Son of God and heard the 'well done' of His Father right at the start of His earthly ministry. Up to the point of His baptism, Jesus had not performed any miracles, nobody had been raised from the dead, no storms had been calmed, no food had been multiplied, no sermons had been preached and nobody had been set free. Nothing of any notable significance had taken place. The moment in history when the Father decided to tell Jesus who He was and that He was well pleased with Him was before His earthly ministry began. This has major implications for us.

Many of us live in a performance-driven culture. Society teaches us in a variety of ways that our identity and significance is dependent on what we do and how we perform. For example, it seems that in British culture, one of the first questions we ask people when we meet them for the first time is what they do for a living. We may then assess the significance of the person based on how valuable society tells us their job is. When children get good grades at school, they make their parents proud and might be rewarded with gifts of money or a special holiday. When children underachieve, they might experience punishment and sanctions, or the withdrawal of love and affection from their parents. Through each of these interactions, and many others, we reinforce that people's value is dependent on how they perform. Sadly, this emphasis on our value and identity being rooted in our performance can also seep into and be reinforced in the church.

We learn over time that in order to feel valued and significant we need to get good at performing. We believe the lie that in order to be loved by God and please Him we need to avoid making mistakes and strive for perfection. If your identity is rooted in your performance, you will only do what you know you can do well so that you can keep feeling good about yourself. You will find it difficult to take risks because risks might result in mistakes, and mistakes will result in you feeling rubbish about yourself. The trouble is, if we avoid taking risks we will struggle to grow in our ability to hear God's voice and see His Kingdom come. In order to be free to take risks and make mistakes we need revelation that our identity and God's pleasure over us is nothing to do with our performance.

Jesus' identity as the beloved Son of God and the Father's pleasure over Him had nothing to do with His performance, and the same is true for us. We are God's beloved sons and daughters, not because of anything we have or have not done, but because of what Jesus did for us on the cross. It is God's grace lavished on us at the cross that gives us incredible value and significance, not our performance. God does not love us more when we pray for someone on the streets or love us less if we miss an opportunity. He is not well pleased with us because of prophetic words we might bring over strangers or because of miracles we might see. God is well pleased with us because we are His sons and daughters and we have been drafted into His family. He loves us, because He loves us, because He loves us!

Little kids are so good at modelling what life could look like if we knew how loved we are and that our identity is not in our performance. Their awareness of how much their parents love them seems to quieten their fear and give them security and confidence. I remember one Sunday morning watching a little girl who must have been no more than three, dancing back and forth across the front of the auditorium during worship. She was oblivious to everyone else except her dad, who was standing over to one side, watching her. Every so often, the little girl would run back to her dad to dance with him before continuing with her own solo routine. It was beautiful to watch and incredibly challenging at the same time. This little girl had no fear of what people might think of her, and she had no concerns about what her dancing looked like. This little girl was totally secure because Daddy was there and she knew that she was loved.

Many of our kids at church are also leading the way when it comes to taking risks to see God's Kingdom come. One of our eight-year-olds got into a conversation with a friend during their RE lesson. They had been paired up to do some work, but instead they got talking about something their teacher had said. The friend said she was not a Christian because she had not been baptised, but our eight-year-old explained that the teacher had got things a bit wrong. She told her friend that although lots of Christians get baptised, that is not what makes them a Christian. She went on to explain that what makes a person a Christian is when they ask Jesus to be their friend forever. This inquisitive friend listened to what was said, and decided she wanted to ask Jesus to be her friend. Our courageous eight-year-old got to pray for her to become a Christian in the middle of their RE lesson.

There is something about learning to be like children, secure in our Father's love that breaks performance and brings freedom to take risks. Really getting to grips with the truth, that our identity is secure and our Father is well pleased with us, changes everything. It means that you can get a word of knowledge totally right and not fall into pride because you know that the only reason you can hear God's voice in the first place is because of His grace. It also means that you can get a word of knowledge totally wrong and not beat yourself up or feel like a failure because you know that you are still the beloved child of God and He is still well pleased with you. Understanding that God's love for you is totally secure and nothing to do with your performance makes taking risks a lot more fun.

We do an activity at TSM as early in the year as possible to try to drive this point home: that taking risks can be fun and making mistakes is not the end of the world. We ask our students to get into pairs and we give them a short amount of time to ask God for a word of knowledge about their partner's bedroom. We make it clear that they cannot just say they see a bed or a window. Instead we encourage them to ask God for more specific information, like colours or defining features. There is often a lot of intense concentration in the room as the students strain to hear from God. We coach them through the activity, encouraging them to have fun and say the first thing that pops into their head.

After both students have had a go at getting a word of knowledge, we ask for a show of hands of who got the word totally wrong. As you can imagine, most of the students' hands go up and there is a lot of laughing around the room. We then have all the students applaud each other for having a go and taking a risk. There are some students who hear God really accurately and we applaud them too. The atmosphere in the room is always a lot lighter after a few goes at this. The students learn it is good to make mistakes, and that hearing from God is meant to be fun. They learn that whether they hear God right or get their word completely wrong, their identity in Christ does not change. They also start to learn about the way God measures success. This is the second key revelation that has really helped me on my journey of taking risks to see God's Kingdom advance.

2) Understand the way God measures success

The way God measures success is totally different to the way we measure success. I once went into Bedford town centre with a friend specifically to look for deaf and blind people to pray for. I had been saying to God for a while that I wanted to see the deaf hear and the blind see in Bedford. God kindly reminded me that in order to see these things I would have to pray for some deaf and blind people. I did not feel brave enough to venture out on my own, so I asked a courageous friend to come with me.

We had a great time during the couple of hours we were out. We had the privilege of praying for an elderly Christian lady who walked with a white cane, and we got to speak to a couple of people in wheelchairs and pray for one of them. At the end of our time, however, we had very little to report. Seemingly nothing had happened, and I went home pretty disappointed.

Later the same day, I decided to go for a walk round my local park to work through some of the disappointment I was feeling. As I was talking to God about what was going on in my heart, I walked past a lady with crutches who was about to sit on a bench. I felt so strongly that I could not just walk past her without at least offering to pray, so I approached her and asked what she had done. I told her I was a Christian and that I believed God loves to heal people, and I asked if she would like me to pray for her. She very politely told me that she was fine as she was, so I thanked her for chatting and went on my way.

As I turned to walk away from her my mind was flooded with thoughts of how I had failed again. I had not seen any evidence of God's Kingdom breaking in the whole day, even though I had taken a number of risks. When I got about five metres away from the lady, the thoughts of failure in my head were suddenly interrupted by very loud applause. In my mind, I heard what sounded like crowds and crowds of people applauding and cheering and celebrating. This had never happened to me before so I asked God what was going on. He told me that what I was hearing was the applause of heaven for me because once again I had taken a risk for Him. It was such an overwhelming moment as I encountered God's pleasure over me in a way I had never experienced before. I felt deeply connected to God as my Father, and freshly aware of His unconditional love for me as I made my way home. Unsurprisingly, I felt a new lightness at the thought of talking to people about Jesus and offering to pray for them on the streets. This was a significant turning point for me.

This revelation has had a huge impact on the way I approach risks, because it has taught me how God measures success. I used to measure success by the outcome of my risks. Did the person get healed? Did I hear God accurately? Did the shop assistant let me pray for her? What I learnt in this moment is that the way God measures success is entirely different. The way God measures success is all to do with our obedience, our willingness to say yes to Him and take some risks to see His Kingdom advance on the earth. The outcome of our obedience is up to Him and those we speak to.

Since this encounter, I try to make it a discipline in my life to listen out for the applause of heaven when I take risks. I remember offering to pray for a teenager who was complaining of pain in her abdomen. I knew God wanted me to speak to her, and I got myself to a place of faith and courage as she walked past us to put her rubbish in the bin. I introduced myself, asked about the pain she had and offered to pray. She was happy for me to pray, and I ended up praying twice. To be honest it was not immediately clear that anything had happened. The pain was just the same as it had been before I commanded it to go. What was immediately clear was that heaven was applauding my obedience. Have you heard the applause of heaven over your life?

GROWING IN OBEDIENCE

God loves it when we are obedient, because it shows Him we are His friends (John 15:14). When you are motivated to live a naturally supernatural life because you love being God's friend, it brings lightness and joy to the journey. Our obedience to God flows out of our relationship with Him.

Sometimes our obedience will be in response to a specific prompting from the Holy Spirit. I have learnt over the years that these promptings can be easily missed or ignored if we do not look out for them. Sadly, they do not come in the form of lightning bolts or loud sirens, but often just a still small voice. At other times, our obedience will be in response to knowing God's heart in a particular situation. Every time we open the Bible, we can see God's heart for His Kingdom to come on the earth. I have often prayed for people for healing on the streets not because of a particular prompt from the Holy Spirit, but because I know God loves to heal the sick. And I will often ask God what He wants to say to people, not because I feel specifically prompted to, but because I know He loves to speak to people's hearts.

Thankfully, grace abounds when we miss opportunities God gives us. I have missed so many opportunities because of fear. On one occasion, I was walking through the town centre asking God to make it very clear to me who He wanted me to pray for. I was feeling increasingly overwhelmed by the need around me, by the amount of obviously ill people. I could have stopped to pray for every third or fourth person, so this time I was asking God to make it really clear. No one stood out to me during the couple of hours I was shopping, so I decided to grab a takeaway coffee before heading home.

As I got to the barista who was going to serve me, she immediately lifted her wrist up to show me a huge blue plaster on her arm. This was it! This was the person God wanted me to pray for. You could not get much clearer than that. As I grappled with fear in my heart, a queue started to form behind me. I asked the barista what she had done, and she told me that she had burned her wrist and then scratched it. I looked at the plaster and then at the barista and then back at the ever-increasing queue, and I made a decision to ignore the very clear prompting of the Holy Spirit. I took my drink, told the barista I hoped she would feel better soon, and left the coffee shop.

As I walked home I texted a couple of friends to tell them I had given in to fear, so that they could speak truth to me where the enemy would want me to believe lies about myself. I also took some time to repent before God for choosing fear over obedience. God is so full of grace. He gave me another opportunity to pray for someone on my walk home. The coffee that reminded me of my disobedience was still hot in my hand. That is the kind of God we serve. If the lie stopping you living a naturally supernatural life is that you have been disobedient too many times, think again. Your opportunity to be obedient and see God's Kingdom come through you is just around the corner.

Living the normal Christian life does involve taking risks. When you understand that your identity as the beloved son or daughter of God is totally secure irrespective of how you perform, walking through fear starts to become fun. When you realise that heaven applauds your obedience to the Holy Spirit, it takes the pressure off having to make something happen or having to produce results. It is inevitable when you take risks that there will be times you feel awkward and embarrassed. You will make mistakes and you might sometimes wish you had never opened your mouth. But these moments will pale into insignificance in comparison to the times your obedience and your risks lead to people encountering the love and kindness of God. These moments are priceless.

The truth is, God is eager to respond to our obedience and the choices we make to walk through fear and take risks. The God of the universe is for us, and with us, and has got our backs. It is His idea that the normal Christian life for every believer involves seeing His Kingdom break out wherever we go. He is not reluctant to release His Kingdom through us, He is not indifferent about it: this is what we are still on the earth to do.

How about you take a risk today? Spend some time asking God what He wants you to do, and then tell a friend what He says so that they can cheer you on and keep you accountable. Over the next few days, keep your eyes peeled for opportunities to do what God has said, and then report back to your friend when you have taken the risk. Remember to celebrate your obedience, irrespective of the outcome. There are opportunities to take risks for God everywhere. Make a decision today to intentionally take some steps out of your comfort zone, and see what the Father will do.

9
KNOW HOW GOD
GETS YOUR ATTENTION

When we first started to intentionally look for opportunities to see God's Kingdom break out in our everyday lives, our naturally supernatural encounters were definitely lacking in the natural department! So much of the time we felt awkward and embarrassed approaching strangers on the streets. A few of us in the church decided to have a go at treasure hunting. Treasure hunting is when you ask God for words of knowledge or 'clues' under different headings of the people you might meet while you are out and about. Many of us felt so much fear approaching strangers, but the clues helped to give us confidence to start up conversations. When you have the clues red coat, black boots and crutches on your piece of paper, and you see a woman wearing a red coat and black boots and walking with crutches, you know that God wants to do something and faith automatically rises. If the woman in the red coat is up for chatting, she too is really encouraged about the fact that God knows her and loves her and has picked her out. Treasure hunting is a fantastic tool to get started in seeing God's Kingdom come in your everyday life.

To be honest, we bumbled our way through a lot of these first encounters. I remember going out treasure hunting with a friend, and after our first encounter her laughing about how fast my words tumbled out as I spoke to the lady. I was petrified talking to a stranger on the streets, and eager for the conversation to end as quickly as possible. Apparently, my fear resulted in me speaking much more quickly than normal. There were many times we approached people and they did not want to talk to us. A friend of mine even had someone run away from her as she went to show her the clues on her 'treasure map'. We learnt so much as we just kept having a go: the best way to start a conversation; how to heal the sick and talk to people about Jesus; how to leave the people God led us to feeling loved by Him and us; how to speak at a normal pace! How to be natural. And as we kept having a go, God started to use us in amazing ways.

I remember doing a treasure hunt with some young people, and one of the guys on the team had the clue 'balloon'. As we turned into the street that would lead us into town, there were balloons everywhere. God has such a funny sense of humour! The balloons were being given out to advertise the reopening of a chiropractic clinic at the bottom of the road. It was difficult to decide which people to speak to, but we ended up chatting to two ladies sitting on the wall outside the clinic. One of them had a painful neck and shoulders, another clue on our map. She had received treatment in the clinic earlier that day, but was still in pain. We offered to pray for her, and she was happy for us to do so. I was very aware of God's presence as we put our hands on her neck and commanded healing to come. The lady said she had a cold feeling go through her spine and then tingling in her neck. We encouraged her to move her neck to see how it felt, and she looked at us with surprise when it became easier to move.

Another time I was treasure hunting in Dublin and a guy on the team got the clues 'yellow' and 'elephant'. He laughed out loud as he was writing down 'elephant', thinking he was probably just making it up. In actual fact, God was speaking. We went to a nearby park that was so big it actually had a zoo in it! We talked to someone by the entrance dressed in an elephant outfit (a pretty surreal experience), but no clues made sense to them, so we made our way to the elephant enclosure.

When we got to the elephant enclosure, there were two women with bright yellow coats on. The second woman we spoke to had pain in her right ankle, another of our clues. She had broken it a few months earlier and it had not healed properly. She was really open to God, and happy for us to pray. As we commanded healing to come in her ankle, all the pain left and she was able to move it with more ease. She was amazed at what had happened, and started to cry as we stayed and explained how much God loved her. We found out later that the only reason this lady was at the elephant enclosure was because her husband, who was somewhere else in the zoo, had called her and encouraged her to go and look at the elephants. She arrived just in time for us to meet her! The way God orchestrates these encounters is incredible.

I could tell you so many more stories of lives that have been impacted as a result of treasure hunting, but I want to share some other lessons we have learnt over the years about how God likes to get our attention when He wants His Kingdom to break in. Treasure hunting was great for opening our eyes to the need around us, and teaching us how eager God is to reveal His love to people. I highly recommend it as a way of getting started if you want to learn to hear God accurately, and see His Kingdom come on the streets. As I have grown in confidence in approaching and speaking to strangers, I am now much more comfortable initiating conversations with people in the moment as the Holy Spirit prompts me. I am definitely not obedient every time and there are still lots of occasions when I give into fear, but I have learnt to recognise some of the ways God gets my attention as I go about my everyday life.

I like to separate the way God gets our attention into two broad categories: recognising when God wants us to approach people, and recognising when God brings people to us. We will talk about how God brings people to us later in the chapter, as these are some of my favourite encounters. First, I want to look at how God might highlight people He wants us to initiate a conversation with.

As a general rule, when I am thinking about speaking to someone I am mindful of approaching people who look like they have a bit of time on their hands. I have found it difficult to love someone really well if they are in a rush and do not have time to chat. This is just a general principle; sometimes God will intentionally direct us to busy people because He wants to meet with them too. The most important thing is to respond to promptings from the Holy Spirit. Here are some ways to recognise when God might be trying to get our attention to approach someone.

1) Be aware of compassion you feel for a person

Sometimes you will be drawn to an individual because you feel compassion for them. In some cases, you will know why you feel compassion, as the difficulties the person is facing in life will be obvious. At other times, you will have no idea why you are suddenly feeling compassion for a complete stranger.

When you feel God's compassion, ask Him how He wants to bless and encourage the person and what He wants to say to them. Jesus was regularly moved with compassion, and God loves to move us in the same way.

A friend of mine was walking into town and saw a lady in front of him struggling to carry her shopping. She stopped to take a break and clearly had pain in her back. When my friend caught up with her, he asked if she was all right and offered to carry her bags. She politely refused. My friend asked about her back and she said she was in a lot of pain. He offered to pray and, to his surprise, she agreed. After a very short prayer, my friend insisted that he help the lady with her shopping as they were both heading in the same direction. She agreed and they walked together for a while. After about five minutes, my friend plucked up the courage to ask the lady how her back was doing. She told him that she had felt heat and tingling when he prayed, and that the pain had totally gone! My friend was able to tell the lady that this was Jesus' way of showing her that He loves her and that she is special to Him. He also got to invite her to church. Compassion for a woman struggling to carry her shopping because of pain in her back led to the offer of practical help, which led to God's Kingdom breaking in. Do not underestimate the power of practical help in seeing God impact people's lives.

On another occasion, one of our TSM students was at the hospital, where she spotted an older lady sitting in a wheelchair who was crying out in pain. She felt a surge of compassion for the lady, and immediately went over to her to see if she could help in any way (I love that compassion can override the part of our brains that makes us too fearful to speak to people). She found out that the lady had recently had knee surgery and she was about to go home but was still in a lot of pain. Our student got to help the lady's husband wheel her to their car. As the husband took the wheelchair back to the hospital, our student stayed with the lady and asked if she could pray for her. The lady immediately gave the student her hands and agreed. As the student prayed for healing and peace, a smile came across this precious lady's face. God brought hope and peace to her just when she needed it.

Compassion is a great indicator that God is trying to get your attention. Avoid just going from task to task when you are out and about. Instead, choose to connect with what you are feeling in your heart.

2) Take note if you see someone more than once during your time out and about

If you see someone in one part of town and then see the same person later somewhere else, take note. It would be easy to conclude that it was just a coincidence, but it could be that God is putting this person in your path again because He wants to bless them.

A friend and I experienced this when we went in to town to practise getting prophetic words for people. God drew my attention to a lady walking past us and later on we saw her again, but in a different part of town. The lady went into a shop, and my friend and I decided to ask God what He wanted to say to encourage and bless her. We both felt Him speak to us, and we waited until she came out of the shop to speak to her.

We explained who we were, and that we felt God had spoken to us about her because He wanted to encourage her. She was really happy for us to share what God had said. As we began to relay God's heart to her, she started to cry. God spoke directly into her situation. God told us that she was a teacher, but that she was having a really tough time with her job and she was really worried about it. She could barely hold it together as we told her that God knew how she felt and had picked her out so that she would know He was with her. We found out later that this lady had only recently arrived in the country from New Zealand, and was feeling very lonely. She was about to start a new job as a supply teacher, and she was really worried about it because she had to leave her previous job under difficult circumstances. Our prophetic words brought incredible comfort to this dear lady just when she needed it.

Next time you go into town, be intentional about noticing the people around you. If you see the same person more than once, take time to ask God what He wants to say to them, and approach them to ask if you can share what He says.

3) Pay attention if you see someone who reminds you of someone else

If you see someone who reminds you of someone else, pay attention. God might want you to start a conversation with them.

One of our TSM students saw a lady at the hospital who reminded her of her boss at work. I asked her what her boss was like, and what she thought about when she pictured her. The student told me that her boss could not have her own children, but that she was incredibly good at being a mum to lots of people. I encouraged the student to go up to the lady and start a conversation with her to see what God opened up.

The student approached the lady and explained she was a Christian. She encouraged the woman for being excellent at loving people and for being like a mum to many. The woman was grateful for the encouragement, and through the course of the conversation was honest about the fact that she was not able to have her own children. As a result of the encounter, we had the privilege of praying for this lady's mother who was ill on one of the hospital wards, and I had the opportunity to pray for the lady and her husband to be able to conceive. As I hugged the lady to say goodbye, she acknowledged through tears that it was God who had sent us to her and her mum.

If you see someone when you are out and about who reminds you of someone else, use what you know of the person they remind you of to be the prompt for what God might want to say.

4) Recognise 'random' pain in your body as you walk past a particular person or area

This is one way to receive a word of knowledge. If you get unexpected pain in your body, ask God who He wants you to speak to, and then ask that person if they have pain in the part of their body God has highlighted. They might not have any pain, but if they do, you have an amazing opportunity to offer to pray.

Once as I was coming out of my local supermarket, my chest became tight and I started to experience shortness of breath. I knew immediately that this was a word of knowledge, but fear got the better of me, so I made my way as quickly as possible to my car so that I did not have to speak to anyone. As I drove out of the car park past an ambulance that had just pulled up, I wondered if the person I was meant to pray for was the one now needing medical attention. I probably should have stopped at that point and gone back, but instead I carried on driving.

What I love about God is that He always gives us more chances to be obedient. As I arrived outside my house, I saw a lady walking up the road towards me, carrying some shopping.

She seemed friendly and I wondered if the word of knowledge was actually for her. I caught up with her and asked if she had a pain in her chest and was struggling to breathe. She did and she was. I explained that I was a Christian and I believed that God had spoken to me about her because He wanted to break in to her life. She thanked me for stopping her and she was more than happy for me to pray. She was visibly moved by the way God knew her and by His kindness in singling her out.

The lady went on to tell me that she had been struggling with her breathing for about six months and was thinking about seeing a doctor. She encountered God as I prayed, and told me later that over the past year she had been searching to see if God was real. I encouraged her that this was God's way of showing her He was. She thanked me again for being brave enough to speak to her, and continued on her way home. I was so glad I responded to the nudge from the Holy Spirit, and I went home thoroughly encouraged.

When it comes to words of knowledge, you can never know if what you feel God is saying is right unless you ask the person. The only way to grow in hearing God accurately is to not give in to the fear of making mistakes and to keep having a go. Be intentional about asking God for words of knowledge, and then find out if what you hear is right. Maybe ask God for a word of knowledge this week, and make a decision to walk though fear to bring it. As you keep having a go, you will grow in your ability to hear God accurately for those you meet in your everyday life.

These are just some of the ways God might try to get our attention when He wants us to initiate conversations with people on the streets. The other way God likes to get our attention is by clearly bringing people to us. These are some of my favourite encounters, when God opens up opportunities for His Kingdom to break in when I am not looking for it or expecting it. Here are some ways to recognise when God might be bringing people to you.

1) Take note if someone starts to speak to you out of the blue

If someone starts a conversation with you for no apparent reason, be aware that God might be setting you up for an encounter. Engage in the conversation while at the same time asking God if there is anything He would like to say to the person that will encourage them or open them up to Him.

This once happened to me in a coffee shop. The lady on the table next to me said hello as she was getting up to leave, because she recognised me from church. She had only been once, but had seen me do an interview up the front. I later found out she had been a Jehovah's Witness for many years but was in the process of re-evaluating what she believed.

This smiley lady was with her daughter and seemed very open to chat. As I engaged in conversation, I began to ask the Holy Spirit what He wanted to say. He started to speak to me about the lady's daughter, that she was struggling to sleep and that the dark evoked quite a lot of fear in her. When I say God started to speak to me, I did not hear an audible voice and there were no fanfares. What actually happened is that the word 'sleep' flashed through my mind and I had a sense that the lady's daughter was fearful at night. I could easily have missed what God was saying if I had not been intentionally listening.

During the course of our conversation I asked if I could share what I felt God was saying, and they both agreed. It turned out to be incredibly accurate, and the lady's daughter agreed to let my friend and I pray. She began to tear up as God drew near with His comfort and peace. I was also able to share a word of knowledge with the lady about God loving her creativity. God spoke to me about her sewing and making cards, being creative with her hands. She told me that she loved being creative, and she seemed very blessed by what God had said. God showed this woman and her daughter that He knew them and He loved them. They left the coffee shop having encountered the goodness of God.

The next Sunday, this lady came up to me at church with a friend of hers. Her friend explained that during the week my 'coffee shop lady' had gone round her house and ended up kneeling on her lounge floor to give her life to Jesus. She had become a Christian that week. Jesus had rescued her! This lady and her daughter (and her daughter's son) are now much-loved members of our church family. Her daughter and grandson have since given their hearts to Jesus, and the whole family are growing in their relationship with God. The coffee shop conversation could have gone so differently if I had not been aware God might be trying to get my attention.

If someone starts to speak to you out of the blue this week, why not try tuning in to what God might want to say to them and then ask them some questions to see if what you have heard is right. God is so eager to reveal Himself to people who do not yet know Him.

2) Be aware of people sitting on the same bench or table as you

If someone sits on the same bench or table as you, it is possible that God has brought them specifically to you because He has a plan to break into their life. Be asking God if there is anything He wants to say to them to encourage and bless them, and be mindful of any opportunities to engage in conversation.

This kind of encounter has happened quite a few times to a friend of mine who regularly spends time in a particular coffee shop. On several occasions, she has had people come and sit at her table, and she has inspiring stories of God breaking in. On one occasion, she invited a lady to sit with her because the coffee shop was so busy. They got talking, and over the course of the conversation the lady told my friend about her Islamic beliefs, and my friend got to talk to her about what she believes as a Christian. When the lady got up to leave, she told my friend she would love to have coffee with her again sometime, and she wrote down her phone number on a piece of paper.

After a few weeks passed, my friend called the lady she had met and they arranged to meet again for coffee. They continued to meet every fortnight for around six months. Every time they met, my friend got to share the gospel with this lady. On one occasion, she got to introduce her to an Iranian Christian friend of hers who was able to share the gospel with her in Farsi. This lady has done an Alpha course, and has had my friend and her husband to her house for a meal. She has told my friend that she wants to open the door to Jesus, but something is holding her back. We are still waiting to find out the conclusion of God's plan for this special woman.

All of this came about because my friend invited someone to sit at her table in a coffee shop and was then prepared for God to open something up. This is a provocation to me. I am often in coffee shops, but my focus is usually on taking time out to be by myself or to hang out with friends. Of course, there is nothing wrong with either of those things, but maybe I also need some intentional coffee shop time in my diary, when I put time aside to see what God wants to orchestrate. Do you have any intentional 'open to anything' God time in your diary?

3) Pay attention if someone starts to tell you about their sickness or a particular pain in their body

If someone starts to speak to you about a sickness they are struggling with or an injury or pain in their body, this is an 'easy' opportunity to offer to pray for them for healing (I say 'easy' because you still have to walk through fear!).

One of my favourite stories of this happening was when a friend of mine was on the London Underground on her way to do outreach at a New Age exhibition. A man she had never met came onto the Tube and sat next to her. Very quickly he started to complain loudly about the arthritic pain in his knees. My friend knew that this was a set-up, but she was on a Tube! Surely she was not going to have to offer to pray for someone on a Tube? I guess God really wanted her to pray, because the knee man kept complaining more and more loudly as the journey progressed. My friend finally plucked up enough courage to offer to pray (I have huge amounts of respect for her). She did not ask the guy whether or not he was healed, so we do not know the end of the story, but I do know that heaven was applauding her obedience.

If someone around you starts to complain about a sickness or pain in their body out of the blue, the likelihood is that you are being set up by God. Ask Him for courage to offer to pray, let His compassion for the person fill your heart, and then see what the Father will do.

4) 'Backed into a corner' encounters

God is so eager for people to know His love, there are times in His kindness that He makes it blatantly obvious who He wants us to speak to and what He wants us to do. It is like He backs us into a corner. These are my very favourite encounters, because they do not give me time to give into fear and they reveal God's brilliant sense of humour.

One of our TSM students was doing a lot of travelling to get to Bedford every week. He had to take his car into the garage for a service and his regular mechanic, who had known him for twenty-five years, and knew he had retired, asked how he was clocking up so many miles. The conversation went a bit like this:

Mechanic: 'You're putting a few miles on here aren't you?'
Student: 'Yes, I'm doing a course in Bedford. I go up on a Thursday and come back on a Friday and it's a 350-mile round trip.'
Mechanic: 'What's the course about?'
Student: (in an attempt to end the conversation) 'Well, imagine sometime in the future you are ill, you need healing, you might ring me up and I might come and pray for you and God might heal you.'
Mechanic: 'What happens if I'm ill now?'

The mechanic went on to tell the student that he had a nagging pain in his shoulder that was there almost all the time. He had been to the hospital and seen a consultant and had a scan, but no one could tell him what was wrong. The conversation continued:

Student: (hesitating) 'Would you like me to pray for you?'
Mechanic: 'Yes.'
Student: 'Wait, are you expectant that God will heal you?'
Mechanic: 'Yes, shouldn't I be?'

The student prayed but then left as quickly as he could, without asking if God had done anything. About three weeks later, he came up with an excuse to have to visit the mechanic again. This time he asked how his shoulder had been. The mechanic explained that about a week after the student had prayed, he was sitting at home and the pain in his shoulder completely disappeared. When the mechanic's partner asked him how pain he had suffered with for years could just disappear, he explained that one of his customers had prayed for him. How would you like this kind of encounter? All we need is a willingness to respond to God as and when He sets us up.

There is no shortage of opportunities to see God's Kingdom break in wherever we go. The stories in this chapter illustrate just some of the ways God might try to get your attention as you go about your everyday life. As you increasingly choose to tune in to the promptings of the Holy Spirit, you will discover other ways God highlights people to you and opens up opportunities for His Kingdom to come.

Many people you meet on the streets will not end up coming to church. Some people may struggle with that and wonder if there is any point to encounters if we never see the person again. My personal conviction is that people are on a journey of faith. If a word of knowledge I bring moves them even half a step closer to Jesus, then it is definitely worth it.

On your journey of living a naturally supernatural life, the most important thing to remember is that it has to flow out of your relationship with the Father. Living the normal Christian life is not about learning formulas or being trained in certain techniques. Living the normal Christian life is about learning to follow Jesus more closely. It is about receiving His love, and giving it away to the people you meet. God is passionate about His Kingdom advancing all over the planet. When you are in love with someone, what is important to them becomes important to you.

Make a decision today to prioritise your relationship with Jesus and watch how passion for His Kingdom begins to stir in your heart. 'Our Father in heaven, hallowed be your name. Your Kingdom come, your will be done, on earth as it is in heaven' (Matthew 6:9,10).

10
NATURALLY SUPERNATURAL:
Lessons learnt along the way

The very first time a group of us went treasure hunting, I felt God speak to me about going to 'Bay 10' at the bus station. We walked briskly through the town to get there, giggling and chatting nervously as we went. I think we all felt intense fear but also anticipation about what God might do. We arrived at the bus station at Bay 1, and as we made our way through the station, our sole focus was on whether a Bay 10 actually existed. As we passed Bays 6 and 7 we could finally see far enough ahead to realise that it did, and our pace quickened. When we got to Bay 10, God made it very clear who we were meant to speak to. There was only one lady sitting alone in the Bay. Instead of stopping to chat to the lady, we all continued to walk straight past her. We had not banked on this actually working, so we had not talked about how we might start a conversation with someone if God picked them out. We huddled together at the end of the bus station to work out who would go and speak to this lady and what they would say. My friend John and I were nominated.

We did not really know how to explain to the lady what we were doing without it sounding really odd, but we felt that we had to be honest with her about God picking her out. We tentatively approached this unsuspecting lady, neither of us wanting to be the one to start a conversation. As we got closer to her we saw that she was reading a Bible, and inside we both breathed a massive sigh of relief. We were very grateful to God for leading us to a Christian for our first encounter. As she looked up to see John and me standing over her, I sat down awkwardly beside her and attempted to explain as naturally as possible why we were there. I bumbled over my words, trying not to read too much into her facial expressions, and John crouched uncomfortably in front of us. God was very kind. We ended up having a great conversation with this faith-filled lady, and she was happy for us to pray for her. I am not sure our prayers were very articulate or full of faith. I was mainly trying to ignore the fact that I was praying for a stranger in a public place. When her bus arrived and she had to go, John and I joined the rest of our group and we had a mini celebration that our treasure hunt had actually worked!

I tell you this story to reiterate that when we started out on this journey of learning how to live a naturally supernatural life, we had no clue what we were doing: We did not know how to initiate conversations with people; we did not know how to hear from God on the streets or share what we felt He was saying without it being really awkward; we were not comfortable praying for people or speaking to unbelievers about Jesus in a natural way. We still have so much to learn, but over the years as we have just kept having a go, we have learnt some helpful lessons. The aim of this chapter is to give you some basic tools to equip you to actually 'do the stuff.'

GETTING WORDS OF KNOWLEDGE

We have found words of knowledge to be a great way of

opening people's hearts to receive from Jesus, both in the church and on the streets. Jesus used a word of knowledge with the Samaritan woman at the well. He knew as a result of revelation that the woman had had five husbands and that the man she was living with was not her husband. What I love about Jesus is that He did not use this insight to condemn her. Instead, He invited her to be real about her situation by asking her to go and get her husband. The result of Jesus' interaction with this woman was that many Samaritans believed in Him. The catalyst for the breakthrough was the word of knowledge. 'Many Samaritans from that town believed in him because of the woman's testimony, "He told me all that I ever did"' (John 4:39).

Words of knowledge speak directly into a person's situation. They reveal something about their past or present that only God could know. Words of knowledge show people that God knows them and that He loves them. I had the privilege of sharing a word of knowledge with a teenager during his first visit to King's Arms. God showed me that this young lad loved to draw and that he had a dream of being an illustrator one day. The word was really accurate. Later in the evening, a friend of mine got to pray for this guy to give his life to Jesus. Words of knowledge are powerful. They get behind people's defences and start to open up cracks in their hearts for God's love to break in.

The truth is that every believer can hear God's voice like this: 'My sheep hear my voice, and I know them, and they follow me' (John 10:27). It is our privilege as sons and daughters of God to hear His voice with increasing accuracy. Of course, there will be times when we get things wrong, so it is important that when we share words of knowledge with people we give them a 'get out'. Using phrases like, 'I think God might be saying' or 'I am practising hearing God's voice; can I share what I feel like He wants to say to you?' will give people room to say that what we have heard is not for them. The key to growing in recognising the voice of God is practice.

There are various different ways you can receive a word of knowledge from God. Here are six that I know about.

1) A picture or impression in your mind

If you were to close your eyes right now and picture your bedroom, how would you see it in your mind? I see the outline of where everything is, but the picture is vague and I could easily miss it if I started thinking about something else. Many of the words of knowledge I get are this kind of vague picture in my mind that I could easily miss or explain away as my own thoughts. I have only learnt that it is God speaking as I have shared what I have seen over the years and people have responded.

A great way to practise getting words of knowledge for healing is to picture the outline of a skeleton in your mind and then ask God to highlight a particular part of the skeleton to show you what He wants to heal. Maybe have a go at this the next time you are heading into town. Ask God while you are still at home to show you something He wants to heal, and then when you are in town keep an eye out for someone suffering with that condition.

2) Words

Some people get words of knowledge by seeing words over people with their eyes open or having words pop randomly into their thoughts. I have not seen words with my eyes open (yet!), but I have had times when the word 'depression' has popped into my head and it has turned out to be a word of knowledge for someone. It would be easy to dismiss these words as 'just random thoughts', but so often God is speaking. As with all words of knowledge, you cannot know if what you are hearing is right if you do not take a risk and share it.

3) A sympathetic pain in your body

Up until a few years ago I did not get words of knowledge like this. I remember Simon talking about the journey he had been on of asking God to give him words of knowledge through sympathetic pain in his body. I decided to ask God to take me on a similar journey. I hoped getting sympathetic pain would make me more confident that the words of knowledge I had were actually right!

It is now very common for me to get words of knowledge for healing this way. Sometimes the sympathetic pain is obvious. I have already written about the time I came out of my local supermarket with shortness of breath and how I then got to a pray for a lady struggling to breathe outside my home. More often, the sympathetic pain is much less obvious. I might get the slightest twinge in one of my ears, or my wrist, or my knee, or whatever. These subtle nudges from the Holy Spirit come and go so quickly and are easy to miss or explain away as your own symptoms. The key is to practise tuning in to what is going on in your body.

Why not have a go this week? Ask God for a sympathetic pain in your body next time you are out and about, and then pay attention to subtle aches and pains. If you feel like God speaks to you, ask Him to draw your attention to the person who needs the healing and then approach them to see if they have any pain. If you get the wrong person the first time round, do not be discouraged. Instead, ask God to highlight someone else to you and try again. Remember that God is looking for obedience.

4) A vision or moving picture

God can give us words of knowledge through still pictures or impressions in our mind. He can also give us words of knowledge through moving pictures in our mind. I mentioned in the chapter about taking risks about the time I got to pray for a man who came to King's Arms having Google-searched 'Backs healed in Bedford'. The moving picture I saw was of him kicking a rugby ball and then immediately holding his back. Some people I know do not just see moving pictures in their mind when their eyes are closed; they also see moving pictures with their eyes open.

5) Dreams

Some people get words of knowledge in their dreams. This is such a great way to hear God's voice. You do not have to worry that you might be adding your own filter to what God is saying, and you get to be asleep! I remember having a dream the night before I went to speak at a ladies' day. In the dream, a lady was auditioning to get into a dance school, but she was unsuccessful and her confidence was crushed. When I woke up, I felt prompted by God to share the dream with the women I was going to speak to. I felt there might be a lady there who wanted to dance in worship, but struggled with confidence. When I shared the dream later in the day, a lady responded who had auditioned for a dance school but had been rejected! She had been so gutted by the outcome that she had struggled to keep pursuing her dream to dance.

God spoke directly into this lady's situation and released her to start dreaming again. I heard recently that she was asked to dance at the front of her church during a worship time one Sunday morning. God is so kind.

6) Remembering

Sometimes God gives us words of knowledge by reminding us of something we have heard or something we have experienced. A friend of mine struggled to sleep one night because of a noisy group of teenagers near her house. The next day she was encouraged to bring a word of knowledge at the front of church. As she was asking God what He wanted to do, He reminded her of the night before. She wondered if there was someone in the room who was struggling to sleep because they were hearing loud voices in their head. When she shared the word, a lady responded and my friend was able to pray that God would break in to her situation. Pay attention to the things you remember as you go about your everyday life. God might be giving you a word of knowledge that will result in His Kingdom breaking in.

The best way to grow in hearing God's voice is to practise, practise, practise. Make the most of every opportunity: If you go out for a meal, ask God for a word of knowledge for the waiter or waitress who serves you; when you go to church, ask God for a word of knowledge for the person you end up sitting next to; next time you buy something in a shop, ask God for a word of knowledge for the person who serves you at the checkout. Then take a risk and share what you think God has said.

An easy and safe way to see if your word of knowledge is

accurate is by asking questions. For example, if you think God is speaking to you about someone having three children, start by simply asking them if they have three children. If you get it wrong, you have not lost anything. If you get it right, you can then explain that God told you, and see how the Holy Spirit leads you from there. God has some words of knowledge adventures for you to go on. You do not have to strain or try really hard to hear Him. You are God's beloved child and so it is second nature for you to hear your Father's voice. Make a decision today to intentionally tune in to what God is saying. There is nothing quite like seeing someone realise that the God of the universe knows them and loves them because you have heard accurately from Him.

HEALING THE SICK

Many non-Christians have no concept of the fact that God can heal them. If you open a conversation by asking an unbeliever if there is anything you can pray for them about, it is unlikely that they will think to mention sickness or pain they are suffering with. If they do mention sickness, it is often in reference to a friend or relative, and usually because they want them to know peace or comfort. On many occasions over the years I have found it surprisingly easy to see people who do not yet know Jesus healed on the streets. There are no hard and fast rules for introducing the concept of healing to unbelievers, and the way you pray does not have to follow a particular pattern. The key is to love the person in front of you and be led by the Holy Spirit. Hopefully the following suggestions will be helpful for kick-starting or adding momentum to your journey of seeing the sick healed on the streets.

1) Start a conversation

You can introduce the subject of healing with non-Christians in many different ways, so here are just some examples. Of course, it is important to start any conversation in a polite and loving way. You can say things like, 'Hi, sorry to bother you…' or 'Hi, my name is… it is so great to meet you.'

If the sickness is obvious: 'I noticed you are walking with crutches. Has anyone ever offered to pray for you for healing before? I'm a Christian and believe God loves to heal people and take their pain away. Would you like me to pray for you?'

If there is no obvious sickness: 'Do you have any pain your body right now? I'm a Christian and believe God wants to take your pain away. Can I pray for you?'

If you have a word of knowledge: 'Do you happen to have a pain in your right wrist?' If they do: 'I feel like God just spoke to me about that because He wants to heal you. Can I pray for you?'

If you are feeling particularly brave, you could just go up to a group of people and ask if any of them need healing. I have friends who have seen God do incredible things as they have done this with groups of teenagers. At this point your dependence on God goes through the roof, but so does the potential for lots of fun.

2) Tell stories to build faith

You might not always have time for this or feel that it is necessary, but it is helpful to have some stories of healing ready to share, just in case. Revelation 19:10 tells us, 'the testimony of Jesus is the spirit of prophecy.' One application of this is that any time we tell a story of what God has done, there is power in the words we speak to create an atmosphere for the same miracle to be duplicated. We have had times as a church when stories have been shared from the front and people listening with the same condition have been healed as God has broken in again. Stories help to raise faith in the person you are about to pray for, and sometimes, more importantly, they help to raise faith in you.

3) Gauge pain levels

It is helpful to have a way of measuring what God does as a result of your prayers. Ask the person you are praying for how they would rate their pain out of ten, if ten was excruciating and one was hardly any. Or, if you are praying for a mobility difficulty, ask the person to show you how much movement they have before you start to pray. As you pray you can then check with the person about any change in their pain level or mobility. Seeing pain decrease or mobility increase is a huge encouragement both for the person and for you. Between prayers, remember to ask the person what God is doing. Pain levels might be the same after your first time praying, but the person might start feeling things like heat, or tingling in their body. Again, this stirs faith and is an encouragement to offer to pray some more.

4) Ask permission to lay hands on the person

'His splendour was like the sunrise; rays flashed from his hand, where his power was hidden' (Habakkuk 3:4, NIV UK 2011). I do not really understand it, but there is often an exchange of power that takes place through our hands as we pray for people. In my experience, people often feel heat in their body where my hand is, because it is my hand that is getting hot! In addition to power being released, I often feel more able to demonstrate love to someone if I put a hand on their shoulder when I pray. Of course, you do not have to lay your hand on someone to see them healed. I once prayed for a middle-aged man who sold fish at a market. We found out that he suffered with a bad back and he agreed for us to pray, but he was behind his stall and we were not allowed to go back there. I ended up praying for him across a stall full of smelly fresh fish. When this market trader bent over to test what God had done, all the pain had gone. Laying hands on people is powerful but it is not essential, and we have to be aware that there will be times when it would be totally inappropriate. As is so often the case, be led by the Holy Spirit in the moment and make your top priority loving the person in front of you.

5) Heal the sick, do not pray for them

Jesus never instructed His disciples to pray for the sick. He gave them authority over every disease and affliction, and then sent them out to heal the sick. As believers we are to take authority over any sickness we come up against and command it to go in Jesus' name. I remember once praying for a man's knee to be healed. I started the prayer by commanding the pain to go in Jesus' name, but then went on to say the same thing in lots of different ways. At the end of my extended prayer, when I asked this guy how his knee was, he told me that the pain had gone the first time I commanded it to. He was just too polite to interrupt me! We do not need to pray long-winded prayers to give Jesus more time to act. Of course, we are called to persevere in prayer, but persevering in prayer with authority is different to praying long prayers because we do not really believe anything will happen.

As you take authority over sickness, you may also feel led by the Holy Spirit to take authority over spiritual oppression.

We do not know how much sickness is caused by spiritual oppression, but some definitely is. As and when you feel prompted, command any spiritual oppression to go in Jesus' name. I have found that using the terminology 'spiritual oppression' is the most loving way to do this. It is not too off-putting for unbelievers, but the demonic spirits know you are talking to them.

An important point to consider on voice levels as we are talking about authority. I have met people who believe that in order to exercise their authority over sickness and spiritual oppression, they have to raise their voice. This is not the case. We do not have authority because of how loud we are; we have authority because of who we are. We do not need to shout or be aggressive with the tone we use.

6) Check what has happened
Do not forget to ask people to check if God has healed them. There have been times when I have prayed for people for healing but then left without asking if God did anything, because I was too afraid they would say no. If the person can test there and then if pain has reduced or mobility has improved, encourage them to do so. It is important to find out what God has done.

7) Leave the person feeling loved
As you get opportunities to pray for people for healing, be asking yourself the question, 'What is the most loving thing I can do right now?' Before you start to pray, ask the person what they would like Jesus to do. We can often assume that we know, but I have met people who are blind and people who are in wheelchairs who have said that they do not want to be

healed. When you pray for someone and they experience some improvement in their condition, do not assume that they will want you to keep praying. We have had many stories over the years of people being healed after the second or third time of praying. On one occasion, a young guy with a bad shoulder did not get healed until my friend had prayed five times! Yet, if a person only wants to be prayed for once, even if you are convinced they will get healed if you pray again, bless them and let them walk away. We cannot guarantee that someone will be healed, although many will be, but we can guarantee that they will be loved.

If the person you pray for is not healed, never tell them it is because they did not have enough faith. I know people who have been told this, and it has left them with a terrible opinion of themselves and a distorted perception of God. Also, never tell someone that they should stop taking their medication as an act of faith. This decision should always be theirs, made in response to what they feel has happened and in conjunction with medical professionals. Comments like these are toxic and do not demonstrate God's love to people. If a person is not healed, reinforce the truth that God loves them and that He picked them out because He wants a relationship with them.

When people do get healed, make the most of the opportunity to ask them what they think about what just happened. Ask them if they have any understanding of who Jesus is and what He has done for them. Ask them if they realise God has revealed Himself to them because He loves them and wants a relationship with them. Look for an opportunity to share the gospel, and ask if they want to give their life to Jesus. If they are not ready for that, invite them to an Alpha course, or an event at your church, or for a coffee with you so that you have more time to chat. It is important not to pressure people into anything. Some people will experience healing and be quick to walk away, and you need to accept that and be releasing. The truth is that God is the one who healed them and He will be the one who saves them too. Our responsibility is to love the person in front of us and be ready to take opportunities the Holy Spirit opens up for us.

SEEING PEOPLE SAVED

I have had the privilege of leading two people all the way through to giving their lives to Jesus on the streets, and both experiences were quite different. One was with a lady I met on her way out of hospital. She had been to church a few times, and in the course of our conversation she talked about wishing she could be free from the guilt she felt about her past. It felt like God flung the door wide open for me to share the gospel.

I asked this precious lady if she realised that Jesus could take all her guilt away. She said that she did. I then asked her if she understood what Jesus had done for her on the cross, and what changes she might need to make to her lifestyle if she gave her life to Him. She had a pretty good understanding, so I asked her if she wanted to give her life to Jesus there and then in the car park. She said yes! A friend and I had the privilege of hearing this broken lady pour her heart out to Jesus as she came into relationship with Him. We then had the joy of praying for the Holy Spirit to come and fill her as Jesus washed her completely clean.

The other encounter was with a teenage girl who came into our prophetic tent with her mum to get a prophetic word. God spoke to me about a reoccurring nightmare she was having about being chased. When I shared the word of knowledge with her, she started to cry; she seemed completely overwhelmed that God would speak so clearly. She let us pray for her that the nightmares would stop, and then I asked her what she thought about the fact that God knew her so intimately. She struggled to know what to say. I told her that God had spoken to me so clearly because He loved her and wanted her to know Him. I asked her if Jesus was standing in front of her, knocking on the door of her heart, would she open it and let Him into her life?[1] She said that she would, so I told her the good news that He was standing there and that what I had shared with her was His way of knocking on her heart. I had the privilege of leading her through a prayer of commitment as she opened her heart to Jesus in Bedford town centre.

Both of these ladies powerfully encountered God's love and made a response to Him, but as far as I know neither of them are currently attending a church. Some people might struggle with that and argue that their responses were probably not genuine. I do not think it is my place to make that judgement. I would obviously love them to be part of a church community, but in the meantime I have to trust that God has got them. He is the only one who can save and He is the only one who really knows what happened in their hearts when they experienced His love. My job in both of these encounters was to be led by the Holy Spirit and then let God do the rest. The truth is that the fields are ripe for harvest and that our God is mighty to save. As you speak to people about Jesus, be expectant for Him to fling the doors wide open for the gospel and then trust the Holy Spirit to lead you. The gospel is powerful.

FOLLOW-UP

Living a naturally supernatural life is not primarily about

one-off encounters of sharing words of knowledge, seeing people healed, or talking to people about Jesus. It is not about satisfying our conscience by ticking an evangelism box. The ultimate desire is to fulfil Jesus' great commission and make disciples of all nations.

It is not always possible to get people's details after an interaction on the streets. Our top priority is that people feel loved and valued. The last thing we want is for them to feel coerced into something they do not feel comfortable with. There have been many occasions when we have seen people healed on the streets and spoken to them about Jesus, but when they have walked away we have never seen them again.

Some people might question whether there is a point to these encounters if the person does not ultimately end up in the church. They might argue that there is definitely no point if in the course of the conversation Jesus is not mentioned at all. Personally, I believe there is a point to every conversation we have, irrespective of the outcome. The truth is that God is in charge of transforming lives. He can use anything and everything to bring about His purposes on the earth. I like to think that when we get to heaven we will be surprised by how many of the people we have spoken to on the streets will be there.

Although we do not force people to give us their details, we are intentional about having cards available for people to fill in if they are happy for us to stay in touch with them. We also have flyers to give to people with information about the church. Our dream is always to see people come along to church where they can connect with other believers and grow in their relationship with God. This has happened on a number of occasions now. We have people plugged into our church family who first encountered God's love on the streets. It is such a privilege to see them grow into men and women of faith who are keen to see God's Kingdom come through them too. We are excited about this happening more and more as Jesus continues to build His church.

There are many ways to be intentional about living a naturally supernatural life, and so many different things you can have a go at on your own, with your family, or with groups of friends. It might feel awkward and clunky at first as you step out of your comfort zone and try new things, but over time you will learn and grow as you make mistakes and experience success. Living a naturally supernatural life will become increasingly natural. As you take the next steps on your journey, remember how extravagantly loved you are. Remember that Jesus loves to back you up when you take risks and that when your motivation is to love the person in front of you, you cannot go far wrong. Most importantly, remember to keep having fun.

The life that Jesus modelled should be the normal Christian life for every believer. My dream is that every Christian in every nation gets convinced that this is true. We do not have to strive or strain to see God's Kingdom come in our everyday lives, because the same Holy Spirit who anointed Jesus now anoints us. As children of the King it is in our nature to have an appetite for the impossible, and it is our privilege to see Jesus made famous on the earth.

My prayer as you come to the end of this book is that you would be catapulted on your journey of pursuing a naturally supernatural life and that your church, and the other believers around you, would be inspired and equipped as a result. Let us be so transformed by the extravagant love God has for us that we cannot help but give it away to every person we meet.

Freely we have received: it is time to freely give!

NOTE

[1] This question is part of something called the 'Miracle Question', a way of approaching people on the streets birthed out of Causeway Coast Vineyard, Coleraine.

APPENDIX
OUTREACH IDEAS

1) TREASURE HUNTING

A great way to grow in confidence if you are full of fear or just starting out on your journey of living a naturally supernatural life. Ask God for words of knowledge under five different headings to create your treasure map: location; name; appearance; ailment; unusual. Then head out in twos or threes to find people who match your clues, and offer to pray for them.

Kevin Dedmon's book, *The Ultimate Treasure Hunt* is the best place to get training in this.

2) ADOPT A BLOCK

A fun way to bless a 'block' of streets in your town. Decide which streets you would like to bless, and then allocate a regular time to be there to see what God opens up. When we did this as part of TSM, we were surprised by how open people were to hear about Jesus. Over the years of adopting blocks, we have done prayer walks, door knocks, carol singing, litter picking, leaflet dropping and gift giving. On several occasions, students have been invited into people's houses to pray.

3) BLESSING BUSINESSES

Similar to adopting a block, but your focus is on blessing a business. One of our TSM teams spent time building relationship with and praying for a car washing company near our church premises. They were at risk of being closed down, so our team prayed with them that their contract would be extended. When the company got the good news that they were guaranteed business for the next few years, our team threw a party for the staff to celebrate. When God's people are around, businesses can be blessed.

4) HEALING ON THE STREETS (HOTS)

A fantastic initiative pioneered by Mark Marx and Causeway Coast Vineyard, Coleraine. Set up some chairs in the town centre next to a big banner with 'Healing' written on it. Invite members of the public to sit on the chairs to receive prayer for healing or anything else they want breakthrough in, and then watch what the Father does.[1]

Mark Marx's book, *Stepping into the Impossible: The Story of Healing on the Streets* is the best place to be inspired and get training for this.[2]

5) PROPHETIC TENT

An intentional way of being able to offer prophetic words to members of the public. Set up a simple gazebo somewhere in the town with a clear sign offering 'Free Spiritual Readings'. (We have found this to be the best language to use to initially meet the public where many of them are at; you might want the sign to say 'Free Prophetic Words'). Explain to people as they come for a 'reading' that you are going to ask God what

He wants to say to them. Help the person to feel safe by telling them that what you share will be encouraging. Talk through the prophetic word with the person to see if it made sense, and leave them room to discard it if necessary. I have been amazed at how hungry people are to hear from God, and how much the prophetic opens them up to Him.

6) PROPHETIC ART

We have found creativity to be a great way of opening the door for God encounters. There are so many different ways you can use prophetic art to reach out to people. I will share just one example to illustrate how powerful it can be. One of our TSM outreach teams decided to go to a coffee shop one afternoon to bless the staff and the business. They spent time drawing prophetic pictures on a piece of paper as they felt led by the Holy Spirit. At the end of their time there, when no one was queuing to order a drink, they shared what they felt God had said with the baristas and the coffee shop owners. One barista in particular was moved to tears as the team shared God's heart with her. The coffee shop owners said that they would put the paper up in their kitchen as a constant reminder of how encouraged they had been that afternoon. Prophetic art is a really effective way to share the love of Jesus with unbelievers.

7) PROPHETIC GIFTS

This is a fun way to practise hearing God's voice while at the same time blessing members of the public. Go into a shop and ask the Holy Spirit to direct you to a particular gift to buy that will bless an individual you are going to meet out on the streets. When you have bought the gift, head out onto the streets to find the person the gift is for. When you find the person, explain to them that God asked you to buy them the gift to bless them, and then see what God opens up.

8) ACTS OF SERVICE

A great way to build a positive relationship with your local authority and bless what they are already doing. Find out areas of need in your town: upkeep of flowerbeds, areas that need painting, litter-picking needs. Volunteer your time and resources as a church to get things done with no strings attached.

NOTES

[1] We have been intentional about connecting with our local council to ask their permission before we set up equipment in the town.

[2] Mark Marx, *Stepping into the Impossible: The Story of Healing on the Streets* (Maidstone, Kent: River Publishing & Media Ltd, 2014).